In His ⋮ ⋮ ⋮ ⋮ ⋮ ⋮ find our life by giving it away to others. What is your God-given passion for serving? What is outside of you and bigger than you that demands your time, talent, and treasure? I encourage you to ponder that as you read Jeff's thoughts in *Wrecked*. The result will be life changing . . . and you may be surprised to discover that the life changed could be yours.

—**DR. WESS STAFFORD**, *president and CEO, Compassion International*

The dissatisfaction we feel has a surprising remedy, and this beautiful book tells us what it is: we need to change, and we need to be broken. The lessons of *Wrecked* will lead you through the wilderness.

—**CHRIS GUILLEBEAU**, *author,* The $100 Startup

A stunning debut, this book—admittedly—wrecked me. In *Wrecked*, Jeff Goins held nothing back, using his poetic writing and passion for change-making to call me to action in my own life. He'll do the same for you.

—**CLAIRE DÍAZ-ORTIZ**, *Social Innovation, Twitter, Inc.*

It's been said, "The true gospel comforts the disturbed and disturbs the comfortable." Jeff reminds us that Jesus not only came to heal broken hearts—but also to shatter the status quo. Let his book be an invitation to say yes to Jesus and then do something daring with your life. May it help you become a holy nonconformist to all the patterns of this world that are out of sync with the upside-down kingdom of God. May it give you the courage to join the revolutionary work of Jesus, loving people back to life and building a new world in the shell of the old one.

—**SHANE CLAIBORNE**, *author, activist, and lover of Jesus,*
  www.facebook.com/ShaneClaiborne

Jeff Goins wrote my favorite kind of book. First he lived it, then he wrote it. The result is a book that everyone who has ever wondered "Is there more to life than this?" should read.

—**JON ACUFF**, *Wall Street Journal bestselling author of* Quitter: Closing the Gap Between Your Day Job & Your Dream Job

Although Jeff Goins writes of his experience working with missionaries and ministry, this is truly a guide to growing up and committing to a worthy cause. Yes, young people will find this book immensely practical and helpful, but so will anyone of any age who wants to do work that matters. Perhaps you are like me, at the stage of life where you wonder if you are chasing air and evaluating your overall purpose and impact—this book is also for you. Get *Wrecked* and walk away changed.

—**CARRIE WILKERSON**, *author,* The Barefoot Executive, *Host of* BarefootExecutive.TV

Jeff Goins has written an inspiring, instructive, exciting, forceful call for young people. I'd love to give it to almost every twentysomething I know.

—**SHAUNA NIEQUIST**, *author of* Cold Tangerines *and* Bittersweet, *www.shaunaniequist.com.*

There is a life that most of us dream of living. Chances are you won't drift into that life. But there are some clear choices you can make along the way to set yourself up to receive all that God has for you. Jeff does a masterful job of gracefully yet purposely helping us take the steps of faith so many of us need to take.

—**PETE WILSON**, *pastor of Cross Point Church, author of* Plan B *and* Empty Promises

With *Wrecked*, Jeff Goins goes way beyond a simple call to action. He gives you a manifesto for getting off the sidelines and living the kind of life you've only dreamed about. Be warned—*Wrecked* will change you! This is one of the best books I've read in a long time.

—**MARK LEE**, *guitarist and founding member of Third Day*

Jeff Goins is a precise and passionate speaker, which is also true of his writing. No unnecessary verbiage—to the point truth that will change our lives. I like that . . . I like that a lot.

—**PATSY CLAIRMONT**, *author,* Stained Glass Hearts

Jeff Goins has written a clear-eyed book about the grit and glory of growing up and choosing commitment over complacency. His perspective is refreshing and at times hard to hear, but it brims with practical wisdom for those who yearn to serve a purpose larger than themselves.

—**IAN MORGAN CRON**, *author,* Jesus, My Father, the CIA, and Me: a Memoir . . . of Sorts

Wrecked is a book you should be deliciously afraid to read because its content will collide into your conscience and derail your future into a life more meaningful than the one you've lived before.

—**SARAH CUNNINGHAM**, *author,* Idea Junkie, *and blogger who tries to bring people together around good things. www.sarahcunningham.org*

Wrecked fulfills two rare deliverables: it messes with you (in a good way), and introduces you to the fantastic writing of a new author you'll certainly be hearing more from.

—**MARK OESTREICHER**, *Partner, The Youth Cartel*

I've read Jeff's writing for years, and I can tell you: what he talks about, he lives. As someone who has given his life to helping the least and less fortunate, he shares his heartrending experiences and struggles in a voice that resonates. Read this book, but be warned: you won't finish it the same way you started it.

—**ANNE JACKSON**, *speaker and author,* Mad Church Disease *and* Permission to Speak Freely

I loved this book. The stories filled me with a desire to be more, risk more, and live more. Who would have guessed that being wrecked is really the beginning to living? If you want to live, get *Wrecked*—read it, then do it!

—**KEN DAVIS**, *author,* Fully Alive, *speaker, and communications trainer*

Wrecked reminded me of my own times of beautiful wrecking, and it wooed me once again toward a sacrificial, joyful life. The stories, the writing, the theology all beckoned me to live intentionally, work hard, and obey Jesus afresh.

—**MARY DEMUTH**, *author,* Everything: What You Gain and What You Give to Become Like Jesus

If you're someone who is groping in the dark without purpose or inspiration, *Wrecked* just might be the flashlight you need, enabling you to see the next step in the journey.

—**FRANK VIOLA**, *author,* From Eternity to Here *and* Jesus Manifesto, *www.frankviola.org*

My dreams and goals have all been sideswiped by something much greater than I could muster up in my dream machine of a brain. So many times we chase and run after a dream and dodge the very things that will get us closer to the dream if we would only allow them to. Jeff has taken stories in this book and wrapped practical advice on what to do when life hits the fan. We think it's over. But it's only just beginning . . .

CARLOS WHITTAKER, *blogger, musician, and creative coach*

In *Wrecked*, Jeff Goins emerges as a noteworthy and influential voice for this generation. As great writers do, he frames the pain that accompanies compassion with words and stories I won't soon forget. Reader beware: change is coming and Jeff Goins holds the megaphone.

—EMILY P. FREEMAN, *author,* Grace for the Good Girl

Everything Jeff Goins writes is purposeful, fervent, and full of humanity. The stories and ideas in this book will break you, shape you, and ultimately fill you.

—MATTHEW PAUL TURNER, *author,* Churched *and* Hear No Evil

If you're looking to be stirred toward something more, encouraged toward your true calling, and challenged to act accordingly, even when it's hard, read *Wrecked* and join the adventure of a lifetime!

—CHERI KEAGGY, *Dove Award–winning singer/songwriter, speaker, blogger*

Wrecked is a creative mix of wit, transparency, and courageous thinking that will catch you off guard and lead you on an unexpected exploration into your own soul and calling. Open this book if you dare to live life to the fullest.

—CHARLES LEE, *CEO of Ideation, and author,* Good Idea. Now What?

The compassion Christ calls us to can sometimes break us in ways that completely wreck our former way of living in our comfortable little worlds. Goins challenges readers to live life not only on purpose but with purpose—remembering that none of us gets a second chance at life. If you are ready to make a difference—a real, raw, life-altering difference in the world—then *Wrecked* is a must-read.

—LORIE NEWMAN, *speaker, orphan advocate, and author,* A Cup of Cold Water in His Name: 60 Ways to Care for the Needy

Jeff has the rare gift of moving hearts. You'll find encouragement, be inspired to step out of your comfort zone, and live with purpose. Enjoy the journey.

—ALLI WORTHINGTON, *founder of Picha Global and BlissDom*

Jeff Goins is one of the freshest writers coming on the scene today. He not only brings a raw, authentic perspective to the issues we struggle with most but also a surprising wisdom that is far beyond his years. *Wrecked* is a must-read because if you haven't been, you will be. And this book is for such a time as this.

—BEN ARMENT, *creator of STORY and Dream Year*

Vulnerable and gritty, *Wrecked* is going to dig into your heart and change you. You will be compelled to live.

—SARAH MAE, *author,* Desperate

In a world that teaches us to spend our lives building hollow monuments to our comfort and success, the message of *Wrecked* rings true: we must allow our monuments to be knocked down in order to make way for something that will endure. *Wrecked* is a guide down a beautiful, broken road, and I'm grateful for it.

—SCOTT MCCLELLAN, *director of Echo Hub and Echo Conference*

Wrecked is one of those books that had me continually saying yes under my breath. Jeff is a great writer whose engaging storytelling resonated deeply with me at every turn of the page. He was able to put in 150 pages the transformational journey we all wrestle with early in life. As a therapist and pastor, this is exactly the type of book I can't wait to put in the hands of the people I counsel and minister to.

—RHETT SMITH, *licensed marriage and family therapist, and author,* The Anxious Christian: Can God Use Your Anxiety for Good?

This life we live isn't meant to be comfortable and easy. We'll all experience and encounter situations that will challenge us to look at the world differently. How we respond will determine the kind of impact we leave. *Wrecked* will inspire anyone who desires to do more with their life.

—CRYSTAL RENAUD, *author,* Dirty Girls Come Clean

In our story-centered culture we've learned that personal growth often comes through pain, struggle, and conflict, but we're still drawn to comfort over calamity. Through his own story of being wrecked, Jeff Goins leads us into a calling of giving our lives away for the sake of God being able to use us for His glory. *Wrecked* is the challenging book needed for upcoming generations looking to find their place in our world.

—**TYLER BRAUN**, *author,* Why Holiness Matters: We've Lost Our Way—But We Can Find It Again

Through the years, I've mentored many young men, but few of them have taken direction like Jeff Goins. His maturity and commitment are exemplary; he is years ahead of his peers. The writing in this book reflects that—a heart of humility and passion and a life that lives it.

—**SETH BARNES**, *executive director,* Adventures in Missions

We're all creatures of habit. We want life to go as planned. Predictable. Neat. Tidy. If that's what you really want, put this book down and walk away. Because Jeff's powerful stories and profound insights will scrape the scales from your eyes and shift your focus outward to a suffering world. The grip on your perfect personal reality will slip, because *Wrecked* will inject it with awareness, compassion, and room for others. Prepare to have your heart dislocated—for the better.

—**TOR CONSTANTINO**, *author,* A Question of Faith, *founder, www.thedailyretort.com*

I better warn you. This book is not going to leave you alone. It hasn't left me alone, even when I wished it would. Jeff writes true things, with heart and integrity, and that's what gets under my skin and into my soul and makes everything get all, well, wrecked. This is the kind of book that people remember reading because it coincides with making big choices. Bravo to Jeff for living it first and then writing it well.

—**ANNIE DOWNS**, *author,* Perfectly Unique, *and writer at www.AnnieBlogs.com*

Wrecked is not your typical book about brokenness. Jeff's writing is deep and poignant. He has written a guide to the life most of us are too timid to live—the one in-between the thrills and adventures. This book will force you to think differently; it did for me.

—**CHAD JARNAGIN**, *songwriter, artist*

Through brilliant storytelling, Jeff captures the heart and soul of those who will not be satisfied with watching others help others. They want to make their days count. In the pages of *Wrecked*, I found a new identity for myself. I want to be wrecked. When you read this book, you will, too.

—RON EDMONDSON, *pastor, leadership consultant, and blogger*

What Jeff talks about in *Wrecked* is more than mere theory. As a twentysomething who has dedicated his life to serving a purpose bigger than himself, he shares the greatest opportunity his generation faces: the opportunity to make a difference. This is a book written from the trenches, and is real and relevant to the real world.

—WAYNE ELSEY, *founder of Soles4Souls, head coach of Wayne Elsey Enterprises*

This book will cause you to take a long overdue look in the mirror. Mired in complacency? Prone to selfish behavior? Yeah, me neither—or so I thought until I read *Wrecked*. Jeff Goins will equip you with the practical steps needed to do something about it. If you're ready to be challenged, read it now. If you're comfortable where you are, read it anyway.

—JEFF BROWN, *award-winning broadcaster*

For some of us, we try so hard to avoid pain in our lives that we avoid making the right choices. We choose to reject God's guidance because we value how we feel more than we value the future God has for us. In *Wrecked*, Jeff reminds us that the struggles we are facing may be the direct results of our prayers for something better in our life.

—ERIC BRYANT, *pastor, Gateway Church in Austin, and author,* Not Like Me:
A Field Guide for Influencing a Diverse World, *www.ericbryant.org*

WRECKED

WRECKED

WHEN A BROKEN WORLD SLAMS
into YOUR COMFORTABLE LIFE

JEFF GOINS

MOODY PUBLISHERS

CHICAGO

All Scripture quotations, unless otherwise indicated, are taken from the *Holy Bible, New International Version*®, NIV®. Copyright ©1973, 1978, 1984 by Biblica, Inc.™ Used by permission of Zondervan. All rights reserved worldwide. www.zondervan .com

Edited by Brandon O'Brien
Cover design: John M. Lucas, DBA Lucas Art & Design
Cover image: Masrerfile 640-02768702n.jpg
Interior design: Smartt Guys design
Author photo: Ashley Goins

Library of Congress Cataloging-in-Publication Data

Goins, Jeff.
Wrecked : when a broken world slams into your comfortable life / Jeff Goins.
    p. cm.
Includes bibliographical references.
ISBN 978-0-8024-0492-3
1. Suffering—Religious aspects—Christianity. 2. Consolation. I. Title.
BV4909.G65 2012
248.8'6--dc23

                        2012019547

We hope you enjoy this book from Moody Publishers. Our goal is to provide high-quality, thought-provoking books and products that connect truth to your real needs and challenges. For more information on other books and products written and produced from a biblical perspective, go to www.moodypublishers.com or write to:

Moody Publishers
820 N. LaSalle Boulevard
Chicago, IL 60610

3 5 7 9 10 8 6 4 2

Printed in the United States of America

For Ashley,
the woman who vowed to be my biggest fan
and has never once broken that promise.
I love you. Thanks for chasing this dream with me.

And for Mrs. Kuntz,
who believed in me as a writer long before I did.
I still have that English paper somewhere. Thank you.

CONTENTS

FOREWORD

One day Jeff Goins pinged me on Twitter and asked if we could get together for coffee and talk about blogging. I almost always decline these kinds of requests, especially from people I don't know. I simply don't have the time if I am going to be faithful to my other commitments.

However, since we live in the same town and since he proposed we meet at the Starbucks a few blocks from my home, I reluctantly agreed. "Sure. How about Thursday at 4:00?" A few days later we met.

A FRIEND AND A FAN

I connected with Jeff immediately, despite the fact he was young enough to be my son. We had a great discussion about blogging, then about life.

The first thing I noticed was that he was smart—*really* smart. He understood intuitively how to connect with people on the web. He also embraced the technology without being a geek. And he was a student of writing. We had read many of the same books.

But Jeff wasn't just smart; he was also wise. Or, to borrow a phrase, "he was an old soul"—someone with a measured perspective on his own life, popular culture, and the world at large. This is something I rarely see, especially in a world where prolonged adolescence is celebrated.

I was also fascinated by his daring spirit. From his work with Adventures in Missions, his travel abroad, and his encounters with the homeless, Jeff was not afraid to step outside of his comfort zone. He had that strange but alluring mix of courage and humility. I liked him.

So began our friendship.

From there, I started following Jeff's blog. I'm not a great writer, but, as a book publisher, I recognize great writing when I see it. I have spent the last thirty years recruiting, coaching, and promoting great authors.

At least two or three times a week, I find myself tweeting out links to Jeff's blog posts. He is one of those writers I want to share with the world. I have candidly told him, "I want to write like you when I grow up."

I guess I have become a fan.

When Jeff told me he was going to write a book on "being wrecked," I was confused. That wasn't a phrase I had heard anyone use. I figured, *It must be a generational thing.* But when Jeff explained the concept to me, I understood.

Until that point, I didn't have a name for it. But I had experienced *being wrecked* the year before Jeff and I met.

MY JOURNEY OUTSIDE THE BUBBLE

In 2009 my wife, Gail, and I traveled to Africa at the invitation of Rich Stearns, president of World Vision. It was our first trip to "the dark continent." We had always wanted to go to Africa; we just never seemed to find the time.

Like Truman Burbank (played by Jim Carrey) in the movie *The Truman Show,* we pretty much lived in a "constructed reality." I had a beautiful wife, five amazing daughters, and a great job. We were prosperous and comfortable. I didn't realize I lived in a bubble.

We spent a week in rural Ethiopia. The poverty was astonishing. We met people who survived on a few dollars a month, others who walked ten miles a day just to get water for their family, and children who had become orphans when their parents had died of AIDS.

Despite all of that, the Ethiopian people remained joyful in the midst of unrelenting hardship. My friend Max Lucado, who was traveling with us, commented, "There are more honest smiles among the poor of Ethiopia than the shopping malls of America." So true.

A WOMAN, A HUT, AND A SMILE

On the last day of our trip we visited a small village and met Wosne, a beautiful woman with a tragic story. Her husband had died suddenly, leaving her with four children in a one-room hut. Without a husband, she had no way to support herself. She grew discouraged and desperate. She prayed God would take her life. Thankfully, God had other plans.

World Vision found sponsors for two of her children. This gave Wosne just enough margin to begin eking out an existence. Over time, she bought some chickens, sold the eggs, and bought more chickens.

Eventually, she was able to buy a cow. She sold the milk and bought more cows. Then, with the help of her children's sponsor, she was able to buy a modest four-room house. It wasn't much by American standards—just a few walls on a dirt floor with a tin roof.

The day we met Wosne she was radiant. Her children encircled her and quietly sat as we spoke through an interpreter. She shared her story of hardship yet beamed as she recounted God's provision for her family.

She had become so prosperous, in fact, she had adopted two other children in the village. She even had a couple of pieces of used furniture and electricity—a single bulb hanging from the ceiling.

By our standards, she was still living in abject poverty. By the standards of her village, however, she was one of its wealthiest citizens.

Max was so moved by her story—and how much she still lacked—he asked, "Wosne, if you could have anything else, what would it be? How can we help you?"

Her answer stunned us.

"Nothing," she declared. "Nothing at all. I have everything I need. I am the happiest woman in the world." And she meant it.

Several of us started weeping. In the space of thirty minutes, our entire worldview was turned on its head.

WRECKED — AND TRANSFORMED

On the flight home, I was pensive and quiet. So was Gail. We couldn't get two sentences out of our mouths without crying. Our experiences in Ethiopia had profoundly affected us. We were, in a word, *wrecked*.

I didn't know what my experience in Ethiopia would mean for our future. I didn't know if I should quit my job and move to Africa, sell my possessions and give the money to the poor, or stay put. Most of all, I didn't want to be sucked back into the bubble of a comfortable life.

Over time, we worked through the implications of this experience for our lives. Not that we have it all figured out. We don't. But we are working hard to make decisions that are countercultural and require courage. In short, being comfortable is no longer enough. We want to make a contribution—in time and for eternity.

AN INVITATION TO BE BRAVE

Jeff's book is one that can help you do the same. It is not designed to make you feel overwhelmed by the world's problems. Nor is it designed to make you feel guilty for not doing enough. No, it's more than this.

It is an invitation to lead a wrecked life—one that is shaken up but transformed by confronting the world's most difficult challenges. It is about living the life we are so often afraid to live. It is about sacrifice and service. It's about stepping into the pain and discovering fulfillment in the most unlikely places.

Jeff uses his considerable writing skills to tell you one story after another. In doing so, he pulls you into a Larger Story, one that requires your participation to be complete.

But know this before you begin: you will need to step out of your comfort zone to live the life you were meant to live. This will require some tough decisions and, quite frankly, courage.

Get ready. You are about to start a great adventure. Are you willing to be brave?

Michael Hyatt
New York Times bestselling author
Chairman, Thomas Nelson Publishers

INTRODUCTION

Not too long ago, my wife and I attended a concert. We saw the Civil Wars play at the Ryman Auditorium, one of our favorite venues in Nashville. It was our anniversary, and we knew of no better way to spend it than seeing one of our favorite bands. Little did I know I was going to get a crash course in sociology and the broken condition of humanity.

For every show at the Ryman, a local printer does a special run of posters that are available only the night of the concert. They usually sell out. We have an entire collection of them in our house, all from various concerts we've seen over the years, each representing a unique memory. That particular night, we were excited about getting the print because it had the date on it—*our* date, the day we were married. There was just one problem: they gave away the last poster to the man standing in line in front of me.

No problem, I thought. *I'll just offer to buy it from him.*

He wasn't interested. Nor were the twenty-five other people I asked. Each time, I would tell them the same sad story: it was our anniversary. Then I would ask them, with a little manipulation, if they were *sure* they didn't want to sell the print. Two dozen people later, I still had no poster. But something strange happened during each rejection. Here's how each went down:

Me: "Hi. Can I buy that print off of you?"

Them: "Nah . . ." (They would say this looking at me like I was crazy.)

Me: "Okay, I understand. No problem. It's just that—well, it's our anniversary." At this point, their eyes would get big. Their grip on the poster would loosen for a moment, and my heart would race. They would look at me with compassion and say softly, "Oh. I'm so sorry." I would nod and wait, expectantly. This was followed by an awkward pause in which I assumed they were trying to decide. I would look at them, and they would stare back at me. Then they'd pause, glance at their poster, and turn back to me without making eye contact to say, "Keep asking around. I'm sure *someone* will help you."

That was the phrase that killed me. Every person told me a version of this, each time with the same sincerity. I honestly believed they meant it. But the more this happened the more hopeless I grew. It seemed everyone was saying, *"I'm sure someone will do the right thing. It's just not me."* Isn't this how life is? We always assume someone else will come to the rescue, but it's never us. Surely *somebody* will have the decency to be the hero. Right? It doesn't work like that. Not when everyone assumes someone else will do the right thing.

I didn't fault those people for not giving me the poster—that was their right. What was puzzling was how they struggled with their consciences before saying no. Only a few flat-out refused. Most just stood there for a moment, puzzled. They would say sorry, that they really wanted to help, and they encouraged me to not give up. It was as if they wanted to give it to me but were afraid. That's what frustrated me. I wanted to say, "Yes, someone can help. *You* can!" But I didn't. I kept asking around, kept getting rejected and feeling depressed the more I talked with people.

It wasn't until the encore of the show that a young woman agreed to sell me her print. At that point, I was incredulous. We had spoken during the intermission, and she struggled like the others to give up the poster. However, she told me to see her before we left. During the last song, I looked up a few rows, hoping to catch her eye as the band thanked the roaring audience. She finally looked down and smiled at me. I raised my eyebrows in an inaudible question, and she nodded. I couldn't believe it; I had all but given up. When I handed my wife the print, she was flabbergasted. In fact, she didn't want to receive it. The gesture was too generous, too surprising. And that's what made it beautiful. I know we're only talking about a poster here—nothing life changing. But at the time, it felt like a lot more than that. Maybe it was. Maybe it was a microcosm of humanity in all its grisliness and glory.

I'm no different from those two dozen people I met that night. I have my own little trinkets I'd rather not give up. I have comforts and addictions I won't let go of. I'm more selfish than I'd like to admit, bent on my own desires and needs more than those of others. Whenever possible, I defer responsibility. I avoid what is right and protect my own interests. If we're honest, many of us are like this. It's human nature to look after your own survival first, even when it's not a matter of life and death. We can't help it. We keep scrambling for scraps from the table, until someone is finally courageous enough to do what that young woman did: to obey our conscience. To stand up and do what is right.

This is a book about brave choices, about ordinary people helping beggars and moving to foreign countries. About listening to that still, small voice whispering, "Life is not about you."

This book is about the most important life change that will ever happen to you, if you let it. I've experienced it myself—at least in part—and it has been anything but comfortable. It's been ugly and hard. I've had to give up my rights and expectations so I could find the life I was longing for. And it looked nothing like what I expected. The strange part? I wouldn't trade it for the world. I *couldn't*. I've been changed from the inside out. I'm no longer the same me. All because of a choice that defined me and continues to shape how I view the world.

I hope you experience two outcomes as you read this book. One, I hope you recall making a choice that caused you to step out of your comfort zone, that allowed you to move past self-ishness and find a life worth living. I hope you tap into that experience and the thrill it gave you. And I hope you learn to live like this more every day. Two, I hope you are faced with a sacrificial decision you've yet to make, one that you may be avoiding or procrastinating. I hope these stories challenge you to be more courageous.

Most of all, though, I hope you're not one of those people saying, "I'm sure *somebody* will help you." I hope you respond to that voice inside of you prompting you to give more and get less. I hope you realize that the "somebody" we're all deferring to is you.

You Must Get
WRECKED

"Something's missing, and I don't know what it is."
— JOHN MAYER

Everyone in this world is searching. Each of us is searching for something to give meaning to life. To bring purpose to our work. We all know this; we're familiar with this emptiness, this longing for *more*.

We're looking for a story to make sense of, a role to play. Despite our best efforts, activities and adventures barely touch the tip of the iceberg. We sense we were made for a great purpose, some cause to make the world a better place. Maybe it's as simple as the realization that our lives aren't a total waste, or maybe it's something more. Whatever the case, most of us despair of ever finding it. It feels so distant, so unattainable.

We begin life with a simple understanding—that our lives are tales worth telling and we have an important part to play. Children understand this: what it means to live and love without condition, to be delighted in. Their lives are full of reckless abandon, and no one has to tell them so. They don't need to be reminded of their crucial roles; they know intuitively. Without prompting, kids know how to dream up adventures and slay dragons. To embark on epic voyages and live out idyllic scenes. To spend hours in the backyard with nothing but their imaginations.

Fixed in my memory is a scene from a day I spent at my grandparents' twenty years ago. I am seven years old, maybe, in the front yard of that old, yellow home, playing on a mild summer day. I am running up and down the stairs, hopping on and off the old, rusty porch swing painted white. In my right hand is a stick, substituting as an imaginary sword, and surrounding me are orcs and goblins and other villainous things. Suddenly, in the heat of battle, I hear a voice: "What are you doing?" It's the neighbor's child—a boy, about the same age as me. I tell him, and he wrinkles his brow, obviously confused. He was an only child, and his parents were practical people. As a result, he missed one of the greatest gifts childhood has to offer. For the rest of the afternoon, I teach the boy how to play, and at the end of the afternoon, he says something that doesn't quite register: "You have a great imagination." I have never considered this, which is the whole point.

As children, most of us needed no prompting to play, to engage in the grand experience of life.

But as adults, many of us do. Somewhere along the journey we lose our way. We get caught up in the pursuit of trivial things. For some, it's money; for others, sex or fame. Some get stuck in the cruel cycle of moralism, endlessly striving to be "good enough." Whatever our fixation, we obsess over it. We give our lives to this pursuit of a promise that eludes us. And we wind up years down the road wondering what happened and why we feel so empty.

This happens at age twenty, forty, or even sixty. Emptiness knows no boundaries.

We would do well to remember that this is strictly an adult problem. Children do not wait all year for two weeks of vacation. They don't spend their lives doing things they hate so they can earn the right to do what they really want. They live life to the full, children do, and somehow we have to regain that innocence.

Something *is* missing. Something important. Something necessary to making a difference in the world. And most of us are afraid to find out what it is. Because we *know*. It's the secret we're afraid to admit: this will cost us our lives.

WHAT IT MEANS TO BE WRECKED

Several years ago, I started helping missionaries tell their stories. It began when I was hired as a staff writer for an organization called Adventures in Missions to teach missionaries how to blog. I assumed this job would be much like my experience as a writing tutor. In college, I met with students every day to go over their papers—to help them learn basic grammar and how to write a thesis. I thought this experience would be similar. What I never expected was how it would change me, how it would affect everything I did, from going to the grocery store to walking down the street.

As I heard these missionaries recount their tales, I realized something: all these people were telling the same story. No matter where they were or what they were doing, the outcome was the same. Whether immersed in aboriginal cultures along the Amazon or surrounded by drug dealers in downtown Philadelphia, whether in the company of dying mothers in central Asia or AIDS-infected babies in Africa, they all sang a similar song: wherever there is pain without explanation, hope amidst despair, redemption in spite of tragedy, that's where they wanted to be. Walking away from each experience, people would tell me how they felt, and they all used the same interesting word: *wrecked.*

Ruined. Devastated. Undone. Their lives were forever changed, and there was no returning to how life used to be. Their paradigms had shifted. Their worldview was infected with a contagion that was spreading to every facet of their life. More than one person told me, "I can't go back to who I was."

> TO BE WRECKED
> IS TO BE
> DISABUSED OF
> THE STATUS QUO.

Take my friend Stephen Proctor, for example. Gifted at using media and video to communicate, Stephen moved to Nashville to pursue a career in the music business. A few years ago, he had the chance to go on an overseas mission trip. He and his business partner, Nate, had just launched their new media company, so this trip made absolutely no sense. He should have been building the business and acquiring new clients. But he felt called to leave. After praying and talking to several friends, he knew he needed to go.

Stephen spent five weeks living in Papua New Guinea. No technology, no access to the outside world—just him and the natives. The experience humbled him. "Life was so simple," he recalled. "Everything was stripped away. God's whisper grew louder to my ears."

When Stephen returned, the trip didn't leave him. It affected every facet of his life, from how he treated strangers on the street to how he conducted business. He wasn't one of those people who goes overseas and turns into a lifelong missionary, but he knew there was a purpose to this experience. He just needed to find it. "I wanted to embrace my passions even more," he said, "and direct them toward a greater purpose." Stephen and his partner, Nate, decided to call their company Grateful Inconvenience, and they live up to that moniker.

Today Stephen travels all over the world producing media and video presentations for some of the world's most popular music acts. Every year he takes off several months to go to China or Africa or the Middle East. It's become part of his life to intentionally disorient himself so that his heart stays sensitive to the needs of the world. He has found his life by "losing" it, all because of an initial uncomfortable experience. Although he's a self-reliant businessman, he still disciplines himself to take time off and serve. He doesn't allow his heart to grow cold. What once wrecked him continues to disorient him because he chooses to let it.

There is something important about a life lived like this— full of moments that tear us apart and break our hearts and help us understand our purpose. Moments that inconvenience us. Moments for which we should be eternally grateful.

When I first encountered this idea of being wrecked, I was surprised to find that missionaries were not the only ones experiencing this attitude of feeling ruined and undone. It came from a variety sources. I heard it from graduate students serving in the public school system. I heard it from friends who worked at summer camps. I even heard it from suburbanites who had experienced a brush with the poor. So I started asking more people, "What wrecks you?" And I was surprised by what I found. Entrepreneurs and homemakers and physical therapists all told me the same thing. They were devastated by the possibility of a better world. They had seen things they couldn't unsee. They were introduced to a way of life that didn't revolve around them, one that intentionally made room for others. And they loved it. They were addicted. After listening to enough stories, so was I.

It was an awakening of sorts for these friends, strangers, and me. We were all coming to grips with the fact that the promises of the American Dream were a disappointment. Like Tyler Durden in *Fight Club*,[1] we were beginning to deconstruct the worldview we had inherited. We were beginning to see the lies we had believed. Was it really enough to strive and pine away for the sake of a paycheck when we had to mortgage our passion? We weren't so sure anymore.

This is what I mean by being "wrecked." To be wrecked is to be disabused of the status quo.

It means to have a transformation that goes beyond mere words—to be introduced to another way of life, to follow in the footsteps of a teacher who is calling you through the eye of a needle. Often it involves being catalyzed by an encounter with pain. The process is horrible and ugly and completely gut-wrenching—and at the same time, beautiful. It is real and hard and true. Most of all, it is necessary.

BEAUTIFULLY BROKEN

Years ago, I was on the streets of Mexico with the same group of missionaries whose stories I was helping tell. But this time I was living the story.

There were four of us in a group: Ryan, Talia, Jenny, and me. We were in Chiapas, the southernmost state in Mexico, and it had been raining for five days straight. After sitting inside for a week, we grew restless and set out to do some good. This was a mission trip, after all, and what did we have to show for it? Nothing. So we went in search of a story, with our own mixed motives, as people often do.

We rounded a corner and there she was, begging in front of a bank: the woman we had passed the other day. We had all seen her and ignored her. We had kept walking. We hadn't time for a crazy beggar lady. But this time was different. Despite the discomfort, we marched right up to her and started talking.

We introduced ourselves and asked her name. She thought for a moment and said she couldn't remember. As she spoke, the Nameless Woman covered her mouth with a blanket; she said it was because of "shame." One moment she would say something lucid, and the next she would get lost in incoherent ramblings.

She was blind in her right eye, which lazily dragged behind when she turned her head to look from one person to the next. As we talked to her, Ryan ran to get some bread and water for her. She would not eat in front of us. The woman complained of pains on her face, but she also talked about having a mustache. It was hard to understand what was real and what was imagined.

After giving her the food, we prayed for the Nameless Woman. She thanked us and said she felt peace. But we walked away feeling terrible. We had prayed, tried to feed this woman without a name, and we felt no satisfaction. This was nothing like what we expected. For all that we could tell, nothing had changed. The Nameless Woman was still hungry, still hurting, and still lonely. And still, we left her.

Talia walked away with an especially heavy burden. Moments later, she burst into tears. "I just feel so helpless," she said. We all felt that way: paralyzed by our inability to help, to heal. It was unnerving. Yet somehow, we knew it was good; maybe not right, but good nonetheless. We didn't understand that our hearts were being changed. This is how it often feels when you're doing the right thing.

We want to explain and understand messy moments like this one. At church or the mall or over dinner, we'll say to our friends that a seed was planted. They'll nod in mock recognition, offering some cliché about how you never know what good was probably done. For me, this has always been unsettling. It feels like patting myself on the back for my own apathy. It's a way to anesthetize the pain, to dull the discomfort of not doing enough. So often we want to move quickly past these moments. We want resolution; we want to justify ourselves. But these are the experiences we need. Our brokenheartedness at the injustices we witness is what gives us compassion. So when we rush past these messy and uncomfortable moments, we take away the experiences that teach us mercy.

Although I didn't realize it that day, the lack of resolution we experienced was a gift. The fact that we walked away from the Nameless Woman unable to help was an epiphany. The world is broken and remains that way, in spite of our efforts to help it. This is beautiful, in a way, because it breaks us of our self-dependency. In a world that refuses to be healed, we must face the fact that we are not the heroes of our stories. It teaches us to rely on something bigger than ourselves and teaches the source of true compassion.

THE KEY TO LIFE'S PURPOSE

Finding your identity and place in the world is not a seven-step program. It is not a tapestry, neatly woven. It is not easy or simple or tidy. In fact, it feels more like a sweater unwinding thread by thread. You are wrecked. It is not something you do. It happens to you. You cannot control it.

To be wrecked begins with an experience that pulls you out of your comfort zone and self-centeredness, whether you want it to or not. Your old narcissistic dreams begin to fade in light of something bigger, something better. The process leaves you battered and broken after the "real world" has slammed up against your ideals a couple dozen times. What's left standing is a new paradigm. It's hard, but it's good. It's incredible and indelible. It's tough, but only in the way that all things worth fighting for are tough. Being wrecked means everything you believe—everything you know about yourself, your world, and your destiny—is now in question. Because you've seen something bigger. And you can't go back. At first the process is disorienting. It calls out the greatest parts of you, the parts you might be afraid of. It tests your courage, the very fibers of your being. This may very well be why we avoid conflict. It calls into question that which we are most afraid of—ourselves. And in the end, you're not who you were before. You're different. You're changed. Your old life begins to make less and less sense in light of your new priorities. Everything that used to matter now feels arbitrary. And it seems futile to try rebuilding the old way of doing life. As confusing or as difficult as that may be, it's good.

This is how my friend Jimmy felt. A Canadian from Ontario who grew up in a good Dutch Reformed family, he's never lacked a theological explanation for anything. The church has quickly resolved any philosophical dilemma he's ever had.

But for Jimmy, that wasn't enough. He didn't want pat answers; he wanted to experience truth.

Last year, Jimmy left on a six-month stint to Latin America. He wasn't exactly sure at the time what he believed about church or God. All he knew was this: life had grown dull. Despite growing up in a polite, middle-class family, his life was missing something. He knew it wasn't actually in the southern hemisphere, but maybe, he hoped, he would find something in the going, in the falling apart. Maybe his heart would break enough that he'd be able to see clearly, to actually feel something.

I spoke with Jimmy the other week. I wanted to know why, at a time when plenty of his friends are buying houses and having babies, he refuses to settle down. His answer was simple: he travels to remember that he's not done yet. The uncertainty of moving around reminds him of the fickleness of life and what's really important.

"When I travel," he told me on a Skype call from Peru, "my problems slide into the context of the rest of the world. Things that were building up at home with work or relationships or whatever become contextual, and it helps me to understand the meaning of those struggles and maybe how to better respond to them. Traveling helps me realize what my preferences are, who my true friends and family are, and where my home is. It gives me a clearer understanding of the need to have an anchor in this uncertain, unsteady life." For Jimmy, the leaving reminds him of the importance of staying.

DYING TO LIVE

I've known a few "cutters"—people who cut themselves with a razor blade or pair of scissors. Unfortunately, this form of self-mutilating is a dangerously growing trend among young adults. However, there is an important lesson to be learned here. I always thought people cut themselves because they were suicidal, that they wanted to die. But in fact the exact opposite is true. Most cutters I know cut themselves not because they want to die, but because they want to live. The world of comfort has slowly crept around them, intoxicating them with a dullness of life that makes everything feel cloudy and confusing. Cutting, in their minds, is the only way to feel alive again.

Although terribly misguided, there is truth in this understanding of pain and life. Coming back to grips with life as it was meant to be lived will hurt. It will bring discomfort. You will have to bear the burdens of others and carry those whose legs can no longer take them where they need to go. You will have to suffer, to endure, to persevere—not just for yourself, but for others. And it will be painful.

We've believed a lie. We've been told life is about us. That if we work hard enough, save enough money, and buy enough stuff, we will eventually be happy. Many of us have done just that, and we are anything but happy. Now, like my friend Jimmy, we are left wondering what to believe. We know something is missing; we just don't know what it is.

Culture taunts us with clues. Through half-truths and false hopes, we stumble upon glimpses of a deeper reality. Movies and music provide evasive hints along the way, but nothing substantial. As a result, our longing grows. We catch a peek once in a while of something that would satisfy, but that is all we get—a glimpse. There one moment and gone the next. All the while, we grow hungry and restless.

This is not hyperbole. We are, in fact, starving. And the only food that will save us is a bitter pill we don't want to swallow.

WHEN DOING GOOD FEELS BAD

I'm a word nerd. In sixth grade, I won the school spelling bee with "acquiescence." Ever since then, I've been pretty fascinated with language. So indulge me the following insight.

The word *compassion* is interesting when you break it down. In English, we tend to relegate it to special acts of service or philanthropy equivalent to the idea of sympathy, of feeling something for someone else. But at its root, compassion means literally "to suffer with."

I'm no Latin student, but I understand the prefix *com* means "with" and *passion* means "suffering" (as in *The Passion of the Christ*. I have Mel Gibson to thank for that revelation). When you put it into those terms, the word carries with it an altogether different connotation. It means more than simply feeling bad for someone else. Could it be that to live truly compassionate lives, we must be willing to suffer ourselves? This is why we struggle to find our way. We live in a world of pain, but few of us have actually engaged it. We are only passing through the pain, without allowing it to leave its mark on us. Emotionally, we are unmoved, and not surprisingly, this is why we stand still. We are paralyzed by news reports and sad stories. Where do we begin? It all feels like too much to take in.

Several winters ago, my friend Paul and I collected some blankets to give away to a community of homeless people in downtown Nashville. When I invited another friend to join us, he scoffed. "You're just doing that because it makes you feel better," he said. That bugged me. Even though I knew it wasn't true, I couldn't shake his comment for some reason.

The following day, Paul and I went downtown. While we distributed blankets and clothes, I took a mental inventory of how I felt. At first I felt pretty good. It was November, and people were appreciative of the blankets. When we left, though, I felt bad. My heart sank when I glanced back to see a group of men and women huddled around a small fire. This group was full of people ranging from ages twenty to fifty. They were scantily clad and shivering. I wanted to do more than provide a few scraps to keep them warm. I knew what we had done was nowhere near enough.

That's when it hit me: this is the beginning of compassion. Not feeling better, but feeling worse. Because you can always do more. You can always give something extra, always meet another need. If your heart doesn't break each time you go to places of poverty and need, then you're probably doing something wrong.

The reality is that anyone who has done work like this will tell you that when you expose yourself to deep need and pain, it feels anything but good. Compassion is messy. It *hurts*. No one ever says this. You never read it on a billboard or one of those red Salvation Army buckets outside the grocery story during Christmastime. But it's true. Doing good feels bad. There's no other way to say it. If you want to get into work that involves helping needy people because you think it will make you feel better, then you had better change career paths. The last thing you will feel is good.

The real road to meaning is dirty and full of jagged rocks. The path is full of pieces of broken glass and cigarette butts. It's long and difficult and not what you would expect. It's not what we would prefer, but it's the only way. Jesus called it the "narrow road." John Bunyan depicted it as a violent struggle to enter paradise.[2] Emily Dickinson wrote in a poem: "Success is counted sweetest / By those who ne'er succeed / To comprehend a nectar / Requires sorest need."[3] Sorest need—ouch. We who are rich with respect to the rest of the world must come to grips with our own poverty if we are going to make a difference. We must allow our hearts to be broken so we can make things whole once again. We must fall apart before we can build up. Anything else is not compassion. It may raise money or impress the neighbors, but it won't satisfy.

THE WAY HOME

If there were another way, I would tell you. I do not like pain. I wish I could bypass this part. But this is what love really looks like. And we know it. "Love hurts," Nazareth sang in an anthem that still makes its way into romantic dramas from time to time.[4] "But sometimes it's a good hurt," Incubus continued years later, "and it feels like I'm alive."[5]

This pain, this discomfort is the key, the answer to our longing. Not for the sake of suffering itself, of course. This is not masochism; it's redemption, making all things new. We are remade in the same way all things are remade. We go back to the place where we began, the place that broke with the universe when we set out to serve ourselves. We return to a garden that was once beautiful and is now filled with briars and thistles. We plead for mercy. And we find ourselves in good company. Because there in the garden lies a man from Nazareth who sweats blood, already pleading on our behalf.

If we are to follow the Jesus who suffered with us and bled for us, we too must suffer. We must hold the dying in our arms. We must shed tears for hungry stomachs, trafficked children, and wandering souls. This is what He wants for us. It's the reason we are called to lay down our nets and take up our crosses to pursue the Suffering Servant. And it's the one thing we will avoid at all costs.

It is not enough to feel bad. Religion to me, has always been the routine of feeling guilty for all the things we should do but don't. We must act. This is where life happens, where we begin to participate in our stories. This is when we awaken. Not on the sidelines; not on the outside looking in. Life is lived right in the midst of all this mess. Incidentally, that's where mercy and the miraculous are found. That's where flowers begin to grow again.

THE BIG QUESTIONS

I do a lot of work with young people—high school and college students and young adults. All of them understand two important truths: 1) "My life has purpose" and 2) "Life is messy." You don't have to convince them that they were made for a purpose or that there is more to life than a nine-to-five job or big fat paycheck. They get it. But where to go from there is a mystery.

If you attempt to provide an easy answer to the question, "What should I do with my life?" they will reject it. Even if it's true. They've seen enough news, read enough blogs, and experienced enough firsthand to know that the world is messed up.

They do not need to be convinced. What they do need is guidance. Certain questions plague us all, and this generation is well aware of those that matter most: "What's my purpose in life?" "Is there really an overarching story?" "Do I have a crucial part to play?"

But there is something else we must ask of ourselves: "What if the purpose of my life is not about me? Am I willing to give up all my dreams, my aspirations and comfort to find it?" Are you willing to pay the cost? This is the pearl of great price, the abundant life we are all seeking and, at the same time, petrified to find. Po Bronson, author of *What Should I Do with My Life?* elaborates on this:

> We are all writing the story of our life. We want to know what it's "about," what are its themes and which theme is on the rise. We demand of it something deeper, or richer, or more substantive. We want to know where we're headed—not to spoil our own ending by ruining the surprise, but we want to ensure that when the ending comes, it won't be shallow. We will have done something. We will not have squandered our time here.[6]

We want our lives to mean something. We want to be able to make our parents and children proud. We want to be able to stand before God with confidence when He asks us how we spent our time here. Maybe accomplishing this is messier than we thought. Maybe something can only be born when something else dies. Maybe our "coming alive" feels like being dragged through the dirt. Maybe you and I are hanging by a thread of grace for most of our lives and we're expected to be humble, not haughty, with the breaks we've been given. Maybe we're supposed to pay good deeds forward. Maybe we're supposed to think *what's in it for me?* far less than we do. Maybe we need to sacrifice more. Maybe it won't feel like a sacrifice at all, but more like the sensation of becoming unnumbed.

It's time, friends. Time to give back. Time to step out and risk more than we want. Time to dream dreams bigger than we imagined. Time to mourn with those who mourn, to bring beauty where there are ashes, to announce a new season in the world. This isn't mere altruism or sympathy; it's more than a tax write-off or publicity stunt. It's a shot at living the lives we were meant to live, that the world needs us to live, that we're scared to live.

IS THIS AS GOOD AS IT GETS?

I love that Jack Nicholson movie where he asks that very question. Really? This is it? All this work and discipline, and this is all we get? A decent place to eke out our seventy or eighty years of life, maybe a dog to keep us company, and that's all? What about life and love and loss? What about drama and stories worth telling our grandchildren? We are all asking this question. And softly our souls whisper, "No. There is more."

We are all searching, waiting for a Moment to come along and wreck us. If we are lucky in this life, our worlds will get turned upside down, our expectations will be shattered, and our stories will shift away from us. If we are lucky. It can be a tragedy or a triumph, but whatever it is, it must attack the way we view the world.

Everyone will not do it. But you can.

If you've been wrecked, you know there is no choice. Not really. You've seen a fourth dimension, collided with a new reality. And there's just no going back to the same you from before. But you do have a choice. You can camp out, trying to relive an old memory or feeling of adventure. Or you can move forward. You can step out into more of the unknown.

CHAPTER 2

You Won't Find Yourself
Where You're
LOOKING

"Who am I? Don't worry. No one knows."

— CHRIS BROGAN

Most people don't know who they are—sounds trite, but it's true. Of course, they aren't willing to admit this. You're probably not; I certainly wasn't. But that doesn't change the reality that most suffer from an identity crisis. They're struggling to find meaning in their lives. They're floundering, lost in a cloud of insignificance and mediocrity.

Admit it: there is no they; there is only we.

We can sense this void, so we make up for it with performance: working late hours at the office, overcommitting to church programs, spending every waking moment on the Internet. We read self-help books and try to overcompensate with activity. We join community groups and Bible studies, subscribe to countless magazines and never read them. We fall in love with romance novels or pornographic films—maybe both. We strive and lust for a life well lived. We long for what we can't have and despair of ever finding it. The process leaves us jaded and cynical.

Why should this come as a surprise? We are searching for meaning in all the wrong places—the places we've all been told to look. Ultimately, though, we end up feeling tired, worn out, and frustrated. And we wonder if we will ever find this abundant life we've been promised.

We are lost. Wandering in a sea of confusion, we grasp for anything steady to hold on to. We pursue pleasure or temporary satisfaction, anything to numb the pain. With our stomachs as gods, where can we be headed but destruction?[7] This is why the current generation of young adults has the highest level of unmarried unions in a long time (probably ever). We know we need community and connection but, ironically, we're not willing to commit to it. We are Jason Bourne—trained and equipped and destined for greatness, but without any idea who we really are. Here's his situation in his own words:

> I can tell you the license plate numbers of all six cars outside. I can tell you that our waitress is left-handed and the guy sitting up at the counter weighs two hundred fifteen pounds and knows how to handle himself. I know the best place to look for a gun is the cab or the gray truck outside, and at this altitude, I can run flat out for a half mile before my hands start shaking. Now why would I know that? How can I know that and not know who I am?"[8]

Can you relate? There may be more going on here than we realize, more to this identity question than we're willing to face.

I recently took a stroll down the "self-help" aisle of our local bookstore, and I was struck with a revelation: this is all wrong. All these books (judging by their titles) were based on one nice but misguided assumption: life is supposed to be comfortable.

We are all looking for our purpose, our calling. Some grand cause that will give our lives meaning. And we're searching in the wrong places. We're pursuing pleasure and painlessness because we think that's where we're most happy. But we're not.

When I think back to my most fulfilled moments in life, I remember often being uncomfortable. I was usually being stretched and tested in some way. As a result of this discomfort, I grew. I make the largest strides forward in life not when I am the most comfortable, but when I am the most alive. This was the one crucial ingredient all these books seemed to be missing: pain.

Phrases like "finding yourself" and "discovering your purpose" have become so cliché they're hard to take seriously. They conjure images of televangelists and salespeople whose hair doesn't move. They remind us of ladies with faces that look like paint-by-number sets (you know who I'm talking about). They immediately cause us to put our guard up. These people and phrases may have the best intentions, but they ultimately fall short of describing life as we know it.

Words like "initiation" and "rite of passage" and "pilgrimage" tend to ring more true to our postmodern ears. But what is our pilgrimage? We have no great war, no epic struggle to embrace, no cause to call out the best in us.

So what do we do instead? We play. Did you know the average age of a gamer is thirty-two?[9] Now, I don't see anything inherently wrong with diversion and games, but that is certainly telling about our culture, isn't it? Instead of raising families or creating culture, we are sitting in our living rooms with our eyes glued to the television, simulating life. We are escapists, cowards, and thieves. We hide, occasionally stealing crumbs from the table of those living the good life. We are avoiding the truth that screams at us from the stillness: "There is more. You are more than this." So we anesthetize the truth with busyness. Maybe if we just do more, this feeling of emptiness will go away. And we won't actually have to do any real work.

INITIATION AND IDENTITY

This really is a modern phenomenon—the longing for understanding oneself and one's role in the world. Ancient cultures and many preindustrial societies all have formal ways in which children become adults. What is the means of initiation in almost every rite of passage? Pain. You walk across a bed of hot coals or kill an animal or give birth to a child. Yes, they can be gory and grotesque, but these acts are what make us more than children. And none of them should be taken lightly.

It's a strange journey, this search for identity in our modern era. And for the first time in history, you can completely avoid it—at least for a while. Like Frodo from *Lord of the Rings*, we step out our front door, not knowing what to expect. "It's a dangerous business," his Uncle Bilbo told him, ". . . going out your door. You step onto the road, and if you don't keep your feet, there's no knowing where you might be swept off to."[10] We don't know what will happen, except that we will be changed. We will grow and be transformed. And it will not be easy.

In this journey on which we're endeavoring, there will be pain. And God willing, there will be compassion. We will come to grips with a deeper sense of who we are. We will do this by learning to look not so much to our own needs and desires, but rather to those of others. And we will find ourselves, one day, wondering how we ever thought another way of living was ever possible.

IT TAKES A MOMENT

Every day, we're looking for meaning. You can see it in people's eyes at the mall, in the products we buy and never use, in the books that crowd our shelves, in the clothes we purchase that never make us look like we dreamed. When we encounter the needs of the world, however, we realize we can be part of something more than an insatiable desire to consume. When we get over our pursuit of self, everything changes. The result is a feeling of being wrecked.

To be wrecked requires a Moment.

In each of our stories, there is a moment when all our priorities and concerns shift. Our identity begins to change. We sense a disparity between what is and what should be. This was what I found most remarkable when I began to tell people's stories of how they got wrecked. At first, I focused on missionaries—people who had been overseas—but as I shared the stories online and in my community, people started approaching me, saying, "I've been wrecked, too. Can I share my story?"

People's lives, I found, were not only being turned upside down in Tanzania, but also in Tacoma. God, it seems, was not only in the business of moving in Budapest, but also in Boston. And that's when I began to realize that this was more than a movement or a good idea. It was, quite possibly, the answer to life's biggest question: What is the point of my life?

Most of us sense a nagging feeling when our souls are quiet and our minds are still. We know that something is wrong with the world and has been for a while. When this Moment happens, that feeling becomes unbearable. We can no longer sit by and watch the world go to hell. We must engage, interact, and be part of the redemption. As a result, we no longer "fit" into the old world, the old way of doing things. We've seen too much, heard too much, lived too much. And we can't go back to ordinary. All of this, though, is the byproduct. The real fruit is what we do with this feeling.

LOSING OURSELVES (ON PURPOSE)

Make no mistake; this is hard. Our culture is so individualistic and wired for success that we often miss the point of life. We think it's about self-actualization, about becoming the best version of ourselves. It's not. It's about losing ourselves.

The journey of any believer is one of unbecoming. "You must unlearn what you have learned," Yoda reminds us. Anyone who isn't willing to leave family and friends isn't fit for the kingdom of God, according to Jesus. We come to faith with a front. As lawyers and policemen and copywriters, we come proud, as if we have something to offer. But we soon learn how little we have in and of ourselves. We must deny ourselves, pick up our crosses, and walk the way of humility, which feels a lot like death. As it turns out, this is the only way to be useful to the world. My friends in the military understand this better than most civilians ever will. Before you can be assimilated into a new way of doing life, your old way must be broken.

I once worked with a woman (whom we'll call Gina). She was a talented, experienced young woman who showed a lot of promise. She was eager to get to work, so we cut some corners in her orientation. However, I was mindful of the fact that our organization was unique. I kept reminding Gina that she needed to get used to our culture. She had always worked in rigid, corporate environments, so this idea was new to her. "I don't understand what you mean," she said. "What could be so different?"

A lot.

Less than a year after hiring her, we let Gina go. There were a lot of reasons for this; however, one reason was I firmly believe she never fully understood the culture. She wasn't able to trade in her old way of doing things for a new one. As a result, it didn't work out.

My friend Matt did the opposite.

Matt and I grew up together in Illinois. He lived across the street from me for years. For most of his youth, Matt was a chubby kid with glasses and a foul mouth. A fat kid with a cynical worldview myself, I could relate to Matt. We became friends: played video games, watched *Wayne's World* too many times, and made fun of the popular crowd. I liked Matt. He didn't mind offending people and had more Nintendo cartridges than the Dali Lama (assuming his holiness is a gamer, of course).

A few years ago, Matt's life started to change. He moved to Seattle to work as an engineer. Not long after moving, he lost his job, which was probably the best thing to happen to him.

I ran into Matt at my wedding, and we caught up for a few minutes. The first thing I noticed was how much he was smiling. What you have to understand about my friend is he was the type of person who said no to just about anything. It didn't matter what the argument was; as far as Matt was concerned, he knew the outcome, and it was negative. But this time was different. Skinny and sans glasses, he look completely different. However, it wasn't just his physical appearance that had changed. There was something about his demeanor, something attractive: he was hopeful.

Matt told me he had starting riding his bike everywhere. After being laid off, he was forced to become more active: to get outside and go on hikes. He started doing more adventurous activities, and he actually liked it, which surprised me. As I listened, I watched him come alive as he shared his passion. I couldn't believe this was the same guy I used to watch reruns of *Seinfeld* with on the weekends.

After the wedding, I called Matt and asked him more pointed questions. "Matt, you've changed," I said. "What happened?"

"I just got tired of being negative all the time," he said. "I realized the world is an exciting, amazing place."

I was dumbstruck. Was this the same kid who couldn't leave his house after school because of all the TV shows he would miss? Matt *had* changed. He had shifted from being a fearful recluse to a courageous adventurer who dared to move across the country, take up cycling, and completely change his life.

We are conditioned to believe life is supposed to be comfortable. But ask anyone like my friend Matt who has radically changed his life, and they'll tell you the best decisions they made were when they were uncomfortable. History's heroes know something the rest of us don't: fear isn't the enemy; inaction is. What we have to learn to do is lean into the things that hold us back, to move through the pain and push forward.

This kind of courage isn't easy. My friend Colleen knows this better than most. She and I met over coffee one night to discuss our passion for the homeless community in Nashville. Her vision was much bigger and better than mine, and this showed. She told me how familiar she was with nearly every shelter in the metro area and that she volunteered somewhere each weeknight. Her life had been broken and realigned to fit around this sole passion. This led to all kinds of sacrifices—some of which weren't very healthy.

Months after that meeting, Colleen and her husband, Chris, took a young woman (whom we'll call Alyssa) into their home. Alyssa was young, maybe eighteen, but she had spent her teenage years as a prostitute, caught up in a brutal cycle of addiction, rebellion, and struggle. Colleen wanted to change that, so she let Alyssa stay with her for a few months. This was a dark season for Colleen. One afternoon while we were having lunch, she confessed to me her frustration with a girl who couldn't—or *wouldn't*—get her act together. Although I applauded her efforts, she shook her head dismissively. "It's hard, Jeff," she said. "Really hard."

One day, Alyssa was gone. Without any notice, she had packed her bags and left—no note, nothing. Colleen knew she wasn't coming back. It broke my friend's heart, but at the same time I imagine it was also a relief. This young girl was a handful for my friend, and the situation was not something she was prepared for.

When I ask Colleen if she would've done it again, she replies without hesitation, "Yes, without a doubt." She doesn't even have to think about it. Apparently, a broken heart isn't enough of a deterrent from doing the right thing, even when it tears your life apart. This is just the beginning of what it means to be wrecked. But it's a good place to start.

THE JOURNEY AWAY FROM US

A few years ago, I had a conversation with a reporter from NPR. She was fascinated with a group of twentysomethings who were leaving on a yearlong mission trip with my organization. In particular, she wanted to know why so many college graduates were interested in traveling and eager to serve strangers.

She seemed skeptical of words like "missionary" and "evangelize." Were these young people actually doing any good? What were they really up to? I told her these missionaries lived in poverty with those they were serving, and I explained how they partnered with local churches and organizations to improve the community. I sensed she was having trouble processing this, and I wasn't doing a very good job of explaining it, so I boiled it down to one basic point: people need to be exposed to pain.

In the United States (and other parts of the world, I'm sure), we are finally beginning to realize how unfulfilling consumerism is. Young adults seem to be grasping this more quickly than most. The generation that's been given everything is seeing the results of excess, and they're disappointed. They've experienced the effects of materialism, and they want more than the promise of property and a fat wallet. As a result, they're turning to unexpected outlets: social justice, philanthropy, and humanitarian work (to name a few).

This generation is tapping into a deep human need—to not merely survive, but to serve and sacrifice for the good of others. From movie stars to athletes, more people are recognizing this core instinct. The altruist within is calling to be let out, and many are scrambling to find their true selves—the compassionate selves they long for.

G. K. Chesterton begins his spiritual classic *Orthodoxy* with an allegory about a yachtsman who leaves England to discover a new world. However, he gets turned around in the process and ends up back where he started. Chesterton doesn't go into detail, but I imagine the man stepping off the boat, not immediately recognizing England. Instead, he is poised for something new, so he sees his homeland with a renewed sense of wonder and awe. He experiences the familiar with new eyes and eager expectation; he appreciates what he once took for granted. But nothing has changed—nothing but the man. Chesterton writes: "What could be more delightful than to have in the same few minutes all the fascinating terrors of going abroad combined with all the humane security of coming home again?"[11] This is the goal and necessary outcome of being wrecked—to see the old with new eyes.

We are on a journey. Like all great voyagers, we know we will discover things about ourselves we didn't know before—if we will journey, that is. If we will be brave enough to set sail, to leave that which is comfortable and depart for a new world. Even if we get turned around in the process and end up on our own doorstep, it will have been worth it, because *we* will have changed.

That's why I don't believe in books and programs. I am even hesitant to present these ideas here, like this. There's something ultimately unfulfilling about a promise of a "better you" that doesn't involve pain and sacrifice. You can't grow without pain; you can't find your life's purpose if you aren't willing to embrace discomfort and join others in their suffering. Simply reading this book won't help. You need to act, too—to do something hard, even dangerous. Because it will change you, and you will find that piece of you lost in the process of growing up, of becoming wise and aware of how the world works. You will become a child again.

WHAT MOTHER TERESA KNOWS THAT YOU DON'T

People who allow their hearts to be broken for the brokenness in the world have something that most of us don't. Compassion. Selflessness. Freedom.

They "get it" in ways that most of us would find envious. There is a distinct clarity of purpose and calling in their lives that is astounding. In the face of suffering, they somehow have learned to shed their narcissism in exchange for a more meaningful life. It is incredibly brave and inspiring.

But what if the deconstructed you never gets fully rebuilt? Are you okay with that? If you are going to be wrecked—truly undone by the pain of a broken world—you had better be. This is a paradoxical goal we're striving for, the antithesis of what we've been programmed to believe. When asked what it was like to have such clarity in her life, Mother Teresa simply responded, "I have never had clarity; what I have always had is trust. So I will pray that you trust God."[12]

Here's a minimanifesto worth committing to memory:

Instead of wanting more, we will strive for less.

Instead of easier, faster, better; we will opt for slow and deliberate. We will take our time.

We will seek first the needs of others and trust that our own will be provided.

We will discipline ourselves to believe.

We will find our lives by losing it.

We will seek the pearl of great price and sacrifice everything for it.

We will become less to gain more.

We cannot become who we are without going through pain. And who can do such a thing without trusting the struggle is worth it? Or that the results will be good? We must endeavor to be wrecked with a deep, reckless faith that confounds the world and maybe even puzzles us at times. It will be worth it.

CHAPTER 3

Help Wanted:
Come and D I E

"I tried to find a cure for the pain...
Oh my Lord, to suffer like you do—it would be a lie to run away."
— JON FOREMAN

My sister Marissa is a sophomore in college. Her first semester at school, she called me, scared to death. "I don't know what I'm supposed to do with my life," she said. "Help!" I told her to calm down and assured her that most people her age are in the same boat. However, I encouraged the questions she was asking, because they're important ones. In fact, without them, most young people are prone to waste a lot of valuable time.

I told Marissa to explore, to try out a few things—classes, majors, extracurricular activities—before she settled on a general theme. College is the perfect time to experiment and fail. (She's a planner, though, so this was hard for her.) Most importantly, I told her to do something unexpected: go where there is pain. "If you want to discover your purpose," I explained, "then you need to hang out in places where there is brokenness."

A few weekends later, my wife and I drove a few hours to the University of Alabama in Birmingham to visit my sister. Over lunch, she told us how she had woken up early that morning and volunteered for a citywide community cleanup. She couldn't stop smiling from ear to ear, and I couldn't have been prouder. She was beginning to understand something that took me a decade to learn: we find our vocations not by focusing on ourselves, but by focusing on others.

Part of correcting our identity problem is figuring out what to do with our lives—what career path to follow, what person to marry, when to take that trip overseas. Those are the wrong questions to ask. The right question is, "What's broken that needs to be fixed?" Usually the solution is you, doing something about it.

When we intersect with the needs of a dying world, we realize our talents, gifts, and passions are not merely ours to enjoy; they are intended as sacrifices. "You think the people of this country exist to provide you with position," the brave William Wallace told a group of cowardly Scottish nobles. "I think your position exists to provide those people with freedom."[13] We who were born into privilege and opportunity were given these gifts with an expectation: to give them away.

THE PARADOX

Unless a seed falls to the ground and dies, it remains a single seed. But if it does die, it multiplies.[14] This is the paradox of life. The more you give, the more you get. You find your life by losing it.

My first experience with this upside-down way of living was in college. I had some friends visiting from out of town and had ten dollars to my name. They were driving cross-country, and I wanted to take care of them. But I was also concerned about blowing my last ten bucks. So I said a prayer for provision, and bought the three of us coffee, exhausting my final few dollars. After that, everywhere I looked people were offering us meals, giving me stuff out of the blue, and anonymously leaving money in places where I would find it. It was bizarre.

The strangest incident was when I found a random envelope pinned to a public message board with my name written on it. Inside the envelope was a ten-dollar bill stuffed between two index cards. Later that night, my friends and I went out to dinner. Without offering, someone picked up the bill. So I did the only logical thing I could think of: I left the waitress a ten-dollar tip.

This is an important principle for living a wrecked life. The more generous you are to others, the more everyday blessings will present themselves in unexpected places. One friend said it like this: "The less stingy you are with the universe, the less stingy it will be with you." This means more than karma. It's about going above and beyond to be generous—as an act of gratitude for the grace we've received. And somehow, paradoxically, our needs are taken care of in the process. Although I still struggle with letting go, I'm learning that the finer things in life cannot be purchased or held on to; they can only be found through giving our lives away.

Of course, this way of living isn't new. It is, in fact, very old, and we are all familiar with it conceptually. But many of us struggle to live it out in reality. As a result, we often feel empty—never satisfied, always searching. Henry David Thoreau once said, "The mass of men lead lives of quiet desperation."[15] Perhaps the reason for this is that we got everything we wanted, and it still wasn't enough.

You've been lied to. You were told that if you worked hard enough, put enough hours in, and got good grades, you'd be happy. You'd finally get your reward, and then you could start really living. You could afford to be a *little* generous, tithing 10 percent to church and helping out the occasional friend down on his luck. But face it: something about this just feels wrong. Trust that feeling.

There is a longing in your heart, an emptiness in your soul waiting to be filled. This feeling is not an accident; it exists as a reminder that there is something more to life than what we can see. It's that nagging sense that Morpheus put into words: "You've been living in a dream world . . ."[16]

We must wake up. If we are going to find our callings, we must live intentionally and audaciously. And we must be generous. This choice is not an easy one, and it doesn't come naturally, but it's how we were meant to live. It's the only way—I'm quite convinced of this—that we can find the satisfaction we've been searching for, the lives we've been dreaming of. And although there are legitimate health, business, and psychological benefits to generous living, the most important one is this: generosity gives your life meaning. But not without a cost.

Oliver Wendell Holmes wrote, "Alas for those that never sing, but die with all their music in them."[17] I've met people like this. People with amazing voices who literally will not sing—not because they don't know the song, but because they're afraid to sing. Apply this to any field, vocation, or passion, and you'll find hordes of people scared to play the hands they've been dealt in life. Do you want to know what the "music" that Holmes talked about is? It's love. Radical, reckless, giving love. The more of it you give, the more you get.

THE COST OF COMPASSION

Sometimes, it feels bad to do good. You never hear this at church or read it below the "DONATE" button on a charity website. But it's true. Just ask anyone who's done relief work or foreign aid. Talk to the staff at your local homeless shelter or a friend who's a social worker. This compassion stuff isn't nice and clean. It's horribly messy, which is precisely what makes it beautiful. This is an essential lesson for anyone who wants to live a compelling story.

Stories worth telling are full of conflict. If you want to live one, pain is inevitable. Remember: compassion means to "suffer with." If you're trying to serve someone in need and it doesn't hurt a little, you're doing something wrong. Sure, it's nice to lend a helping hand, but true compassion causes your heart to break—even at the moment you're helping. It breaks for all the needs you're not meeting, for everything else you could be doing. When you hold the dying in your arms, when you put a pair of shoes on someone's bare feet, when you listen to a homeless person's story—these things don't feel good. They hurt. Which is what they're supposed to do. They remind us of a world that is still broken, that still needs to be healed.

When people say the only reason to help the less fortunate is so you can feel better about yourself, I laugh. Those people obviously have never lived among the poor, the destitute, the heartbroken. They have never put themselves out there and truly suffered with someone in pain. This idea that philanthropy is self-medication is not true; in fact, it's so outrageous that it's laughable. If you're really helping someone in pain—if you're really experiencing compassion—you can't help but hurt, too.

This is the litmus test for those aspiring to make a difference in others' lives: Do we feel cheery about the work we're doing, or does it hurt a little, maybe even a lot? If the latter, you're on the right track. Listen. This is not Disney World; it's the *real* world. This is life—real and raw and gritty, full of all the things you'd rather not see. And if you are going to change something, you are going to have to enter into the brokenness and experience some of the pain therein. The only escape from this reality is to live only for yourself. And we all know what that gets us: exactly what we already have.

Serving others so we feel better about ourselves is not the same as compassion, and this is a crucial distinction. Because when you set out to find your calling, you will encounter counterfeits: organizations and opportunities that pander to your narcissism, promising a better feeling in exchange for a few service hours. I promise you that this is not the life God intended for you. When you see such promises, run.

On the other hand, there is nothing wrong with the satisfaction that comes from finding your life's work. Again, we experience a paradox. Entering the pain of others can make us feel good, giving us a deep confidence about our place in the world, while doing work that doesn't feel good at all. In other words, in our grief, we find purpose. In suffering, we find significance. And still, the pain goes on.

The intersection between these two contradictions is where we find our true selves.

THE GREAT CLICHÉ

My friend Dustin grew up in a nice, middle-class family in central Illinois. He made good grades, played sports, and tried to be a moral person. Then college happened. During his freshmen year, he was a wild man. Parties. Drinking. Girls. You name it—he did it. College was hard. Even after he became a born-again Christian and started turning his life around, Dustin's memories of school are filled with feelings of regret and self-doubt.

It wasn't until Dustin moved to Guatemala that his life began to change, that he truly started to understand what he was made to do. Even then, it happened in an odd, roundabout way.

Dustin spent two years in Quetzaltenango as an English teacher at a school for college-bound Guatemalans. There he discovered two passions: first was Spanish, and second his love for teaching. He also saw poverty in Guatemala like he had never before seen in his life. And all of this collectively influenced his worldview.

After a two-year stint in Latin America, Dustin came home to get married and move to Oklahoma. He thought his forays into education and foreign language were complete. Now it was time to move on, to grow up. So he tried different things: selling insurance, working in an international sales office, getting people to purchase gym memberships. He always had the ability to persuade; that was something I admired about him. For a season, he tried to use this gift to make a living, but that wasn't how God had wired him. He bounced from one short-term commitment to the next, always convinced that "this was it" and ultimately left with that feeling of wanting something more. When his wife, Kristen, finished medical school, they both took a job at a clinic where he was able to settle his spirit for a season. However, this only lasted about six months. Then he was on to his next job, which was selling chemicals. Something was missing for my friend, and he didn't know what it was. Nothing felt good enough or big enough for his desires. This frustrated him, but he didn't know what to do with it.

Dustin had always been adventurous. He had a tattoo on his back and wasn't afraid of jumping off a bridge now and then. Frankly, his courage both inspired and intimidated me. Our favorite taunt in school was "you're not crazy enough to . . ." and whatever we finished the sentence with, he would do. It was a cruel game we played, usually for our own amusement. So it wasn't that much of a surprise when Dustin called me to tell me he and Kristen were leaving their jobs to leave the country—and they would be leaving in a matter of months. Only this time, I wasn't there to egg him on. He must've dared himself.

Through an interesting turn of events, the school in Guatemala where Dustin had worked for two years after college was in need of some last-minute help. To his delight, Kristen was excited about the prospect, and they both signed a contract for a year. He was able to introduce his wife to the country he had fallen in love with years before, and Kristen was able to have an adventure of her own. It was the promise of everything they had hoped for, a journey they could finally share—but it didn't turn out like they expected.

Halfway through the year, Dustin and Kristen had to break their commitment to the school and move back home. There were some family issues, and it was the right thing to do, but still hard. In Dustin's mind, even though he knew better, it felt like failure. Like giving up. But through it, he learned a crucial lesson. Before leaving Central America, he took a two-week hike through the jungle with a friend. It was a pilgrimage of sorts—a journey to discover what he wanted out of life and to mourn the lost dream of living in Guatemala with his wife.

Somewhere out in the jungle, God spoke to Dustin. According to him, he almost died a few times on the trip, which allowed him to gain the perspective he was lacking. For one, he realized how tired he was of moving all the time. At age twenty-nine, he had lived in three different countries, three different states, and seven different cities as an adult. He had had more than ten different jobs and virtually no "roots" established. His restlessness had finally caught up with him. So he made a commitment. Miles away from civilization, he resolved, "No matter where the road may lead, my intention was to stay, build roots, join a tribe, start a family, and stop looking ahead to the next move."

When Dustin returned home, he was a new man. He and Kristen returned to Oklahoma, where he found a job as a high school Spanish teacher. Although it took years of travel and searching and a lot of pain and disappointment, Dustin finally found what he was looking for. It wasn't as glamorous or adventurous as he thought, but it was fulfilling. He found his true passion: not traveling, but teaching. It happened in a roundabout way, but the only way it could have.

If you are going to find work worth doing—a vocation to fulfill and challenge you—you will have to encounter a reality bigger than yourself. It may not be what others say it should be or what you think, but it will come if you are looking for it. Our callings come to us as surprises, like a distant dream we could've sworn was real. When you find it, whatever your "it" is, it will be unavoidable—something that wrecks you and compels you to act. At times, the work you're called to do will be hard and confusing, but if you press in, you will see the purpose behind the pain. You will see how the whole experience is causing you to grow. And you will thank God for the whole journey.

Every journey brings with it sacrifice; it's what makes the destination worthwhile. For Dustin, this meant giving up his natural ability to sell and persuade, which ultimately led him to another country, a place of poverty, where he found a need that was actually quite close to home. The difference was he had to go to find it. What I'm trying to say is this: it's hard to get your heart broken on the couch. You have to go. To search. To journey. You have to learn to live an adventure, and all the best ones ultimately lead you home. Yes, finding yourself is a cliché, but the language is right. This will take courage and some sort of voyage—a finding of sorts. The real you is out there, waiting to be discovered.

Our callings and identities are interwoven. They're not the same, but they are linked. We find out who we are in the context of what we do. It's impossible to know who you are without moving in some direction. Dustin thought he knew who he was but wasn't sure how he should be using his gifts. The reality, though, is he learned a lot about himself from the journey, culminating in a vocation that stuck. The same is true for anyone eager to find their place in the world. Your calling is out there, quite possibly hidden in the dark and broken places of the world. It's your job to find it.

CHAPTER 4

How I was
WRECKED

"We, the willing, led by the unknowing, are doing the impossible for the ungrateful. We have done so much, for so long, with so little, we are now qualified to do anything with nothing."

— MOTHER TERESA

It's the unfamiliar that calls us to be more than we can be on our own. It starts as a whisper, then grows to a scream. Those of us who will venture out into the world with ears open will eventually hear something. It may lure us like a song or send us to the ground like an air-raid siren. But it will come, and it will be unmistakable. If we are willing, we will be wrecked.

My first experience with being wrecked was in college. I was in Spain on a study abroad program and was caught in my own world of travel and education. It began one night when I did something completely different. I decided to turn around.

"I COULD BE DEAD TOMORROW!"

It was junior year of college, and I spent most days in class and most evenings hopping from one flamenco bar to the next.

Adopting the name *Pepe* (which was ironic for a pasty redhead from the Midwest), I immersed myself fully into Spanish culture. With a leather satchel from Florence, black leather shoes from *El Corte Ingles*, and a growing Andalusian lisp, I was determined to blend into the sea of olive skin around me. By the end of each night, I had learned another phrase I was eager to use in class the next day, usually mortifying my professors. That was a typical day-in-the-life of a wannabe Spaniard.

One evening, though, the typical took an unexpected turn.

On this particular night, as my friends and I were leaving the school and trying to figure out what we were going to do for the evening, we were interrupted by a whisper: "Pssst!"

Standing in the middle of the street contemplating our plans for the evening, we didn't notice it at first. Caught up in our excitement of exploring the city, we continued chatting. Would it be the same bar we had frequented the last few nights, or would we dare to attend a *discoteca*? We decided to head back to our host homes and temporarily suspend our plans until after supper, so we started walking. We headed in the direction of the bridge that crossed the Guadalquivir River, which we traversed every day.

The voice came again, forming actual words this time: "Hey you!"

This time, we stopped, turned around, and saw him emerge from the alley. The man was wearing a white shirt and brown pants, both covered in a sooty material. Rugged and gruff, he stood at least six feet in the air. His dirty, cracked hands stroked a gray beard, stained yellow around his mouth. Holes had worn through his old dress pants, exposing his hairy knees, and his button-down shirt was scattered with stains. To cover it all, he wore a large brown jacket. It was obvious: this man was a vagrant. "*Vagabundos*," my host mom called them. Not the type we should associate with, we were told.

He said something in broken Spanish, which caught our attention, so we turned around. We all stared at him, confused. He was too pasty to be Spanish, too cultured-looking to be American. No one said anything. We just gawked. Try as we might, we were unable to place the man; something didn't fit. He spoke again in French, his voice beginning to crack. Then he commanded our attention with a harsh slur of words we didn't recognize. What was that—German? Still, we said nothing.

Finally, one of us broke the silence.

"What's the matter?" Lucretia asked. She was part Guatemalan and had been living in Seville for over a year now, making her practically a native in our eyes. Not to mention she worked with the study abroad program, so it seemed natural to let her do the talking.

The man said he needed money and asked if she would be willing to help. He said he had no place to go, no place to stay. Nowhere to lay his head. My friends and I looked at each other uneasily. We had just come from a Bible study, where we had discussed how we were acclimating to a new culture and city. Most of us were from the suburbs or had grown up in rural farming communities, and the transition was a little jarring.

This was the first time anything like this had ever happened to me. In northern Illinois, we didn't have homeless people. At least none that I recall seeing. But this was Seville—a city accustomed to passersby and vagrants and refugees. These kinds of things happened every day here.

Again, Lucretia was the brave one: "I don't have any cash on me. Will you be here tomorrow?"

"I don't know where I'll be tomorrow," he replied.

Of course you don't, I thought. *You're homeless.*

"Tomorrow doesn't exist for me. I could be here, there, any-where. I could be dead tomorrow! In the name of Jesus Christ, help me," he pleaded. "Please, I love God. I just need some food."

As soon as they left his lips, the words struck me hard. But I stood motionless, watching him. I felt paralyzed. But what could I do?

Lucretia played the diplomat well. She promised to return, but the man wasn't satisfied. He screamed after us as we walked away, saying things about God, about Jesus—anything to cause us to turn around. Even after we turned to cross the bridge, his words hung in my mind, plaguing me. But we kept moving anyway.

Attempting to drown out the man's unrelenting cries, we distracted ourselves with idle conversation. I talked with my roommate about what he thought our host mom had prepared for supper. He replied, trying to fill the awkwardness we all felt, trying to silence our consciences. But all I could hear were the desperate pleas of a vagrant in need. Even when we neared the other side of the river, the sounds were impossible to ignore.

By the time we were halfway across the bridge, my stomach was churning. There was a heaviness in my heart I couldn't shake. The cries had now ceased, but I was starting to feel ill. And despite my best efforts to avoid the guilt, the man's words continued to echo in my soul.

In the name of Jesus Christ . . .

I kept walking, each step getting heavier, a little more miser-able than the last.

In the name of . . .

Finally, I couldn't take it anymore. I tossed my backpack at my roommate with an ambiguous explanation: "Just something I need to take care of," I muttered. Then, I turned around. And ran.

Racing across the bridge, I dodged men and women who were

walking home from work. They glared at me, the white tourist bounding past them with determination. Each stride was longer than the last, and my heart beat quickly—I couldn't get there soon enough.

Arriving on the other side of the river, I searched the crowd. The man was nowhere to be found. I worried he had already moved on to another square, on to another audience who would ignore him.

But then I saw him crouched in the alley next to our school, smoking a cigarette.

Due to a lack of exposure, I had a general distrust of homeless people. I was afraid of them. I was, therefore, by no means going to fork over a bunch of cash to some European loudmouth. I was too smart for that, or maybe too cold. Still, I knew I had to do something. So I did what I knew how to do. I fed the man.

"Are you hungry?" I asked, halfheartedly. It was more of a demand than a question. He nodded slowly. "Then follow me."

McDonald's was on the corner, so it was a convenient place to stop. *An in-and-out trip*, I thought. *No hassle, no drama*. I told the man to sit in one of the yellow booths and asked what he wanted. He gave his order: cheeseburger, fries, and a beer.

"I'm sorry about that," he said, embarrassed. "But I really want one."

"Don't worry about it," I said, smiling for the first time since leaving the school. I walked over to the line.

A few minutes later, I returned to the booth with a tray of food. I watched him quickly devour his meal, and neither of us said a word.

After a long swig of beer, he asked my name, and I told him.

"Micah," he returned, slapping his chest like a caveman. He asked what I was doing here. I told him we were all students and the school where we studied was in the building he saw us leaving.

Then I asked Micah's story. He only told me bits and pieces, but I did my best to connect them.

Micah came to Seville from Germany but couldn't return now. He had been kicked out of the country—for what, I couldn't understand. He would've gone back, he told me, if it weren't for one little issue: he had lost his papers. Without them, it was impossible to get home. So here he was, stuck in limbo, doomed to wander.

Every night, Micah tried to scrape together enough change to eat a hot meal. Most nights, he was lucky—he'd find something in a dumpster or left on a park bench. A sandwich, a loaf of bread, an apple. But tonight was different.

As he spoke, he got pieces of burger stuck in his ragged beard. Between chews, he would say something in broken English I could barely understand, and then he'd smile the biggest grin in all of Europe. And of course, I would smile back. We talked like this— back and forth—for about an hour. Just sharing our lives with each other: our interests, passions, and struggles. We listened and learned from each other, and as we did, we both became human. He was no longer the scary beggar, and I was no longer the heart-less, selfish American from an hour before.

Then Micah told me something that shocked me, something that truly wrecked me.

"Jeff, I speak to so many people, so many every day, and you are the only one." I raised an eyebrow as he paused, unsure of what he meant. "The only one who stopped. The only one who did anything for me. Why did you come back?"

I swallowed hard in disbelief. *The only one? Really?* And I had only showed up out of guilt. *Surely, somebody else had stopped to help at some point . . . right?*

"Well," I said, "I guess it's what you said about not knowing if you'll live until tomorrow and all that stuff about Jesus. That's what He would have done, I think." In retrospect, I should have been better prepared for this question. I should have rehearsed it ahead of time and been ready with an important theological retort. I felt I had failed my new friend, but he seemed to think it was adequate, nodding and stuffing a handful of food into his mouth.

"I love God," he said through a mouthful of fries. And I believed him.

All the way home, I couldn't stop smiling. I couldn't recall the last time I felt so alive, the last time I felt so free. I had passed people on the street before, I was sure of it. My usual response was to ignore them, to pretend I didn't see. I thought this was wise, that I was showing discernment. But the truth was I was scared. For years, I was trapped by fear, paralyzed from doing the right thing. Stuck in a life that was more about me than others. That night, though, something changed. Something good and true was shaken loose, and I didn't want to lose it. As I walked home, I thanked God for the opportunity I had almost missed, for the smile on my face I couldn't wipe off. For the blood racing through my veins and the fact that Micah's belly was full tonight.

I never saw him again, even though I hoped I would. I wondered if he found a meal the next night. And the next night. And the one after that. I thought about him often, wondering how he was doing, if he was surviving. After that night, I made a habit of asking my host mom for two sandwiches for lunch, just in case I ran into Micah or someone like him. And of course, I did. I ran into all kinds of people—people I had never noticed before that were now impossible to ignore. The gypsy woman who sat on the steps of the cathedral. The paraplegic outside the museum.

The dark-skinned family in the park that looked more Arab than Spanish. I was finally starting to see.

It wasn't just Seville that was suddenly teeming with people who had been marginalized. Returning to the United States, I had a heightened awareness of the unseen, a call to the unfamiliar that stuck with me.

ODE TO A SHOE-SHINER

When I first moved to Nashville, I didn't have a job. Between interviews, I would take trips to downtown to walk off stress and anxiety. I was coming up empty so far in my job search and worried I would never get out of my parents' house. I was still concerned about myself, about my own preservation.

One overcast afternoon, I found myself feeling defeated from my failed job search. So I set out to go exploring. The weather called for chance of ran, but I hit the streets anyway. I saw some homeless people from my car and thought I should talk to them or give them food or money or something. From the comfort of my car, I thought this.

I parked and went in search of them, in search of doing something good, albeit comfortable.

I passed one person poorly dressed, but he wasn't begging. *Maybe he wasn't homeless?* Another guy was eating in a bus stop. *Maybe he's just waiting to go home?* Then there was a group of raggedly dressed people who were conversing with someone in much nicer clothes. Someone beat me to the punch. I passed a few more, continuing to make excuses for not stopping. I felt defeated by my own apathy and started to beat myself up. All the while, $1.50 in change jingled in my suit coat, completely useless. I had even planned how much I would give so it wouldn't be impulsive. "God loves a cheerful giver," after all. I was a failure. Dejected and despairing, I turned around and headed back toward my vehicle after half an hour of walking around.

A few blocks from my car, I rounded the corner, and then I heard it:

"Shoe shine, sir?" The voice was soft and calm, without a hint of crazy. I looked up to see a man on his knees with several bottles of black and brown shoe polish, some toothbrushes, and a few dirty rags beside him. He had his whole shop set up on the street corner.

"How much?" I asked suspiciously. The generous me had departed. Reason had returned. I had no job, after all, and money was tight.

"Whatever you think it's worth," was the humble reply.

Blessed are the meek.

"Okay," I replied. And he went to work.

The grey, foreboding storm clouds finally gave way, and it started to rain. The man began moving things to get me under some shelter. I told him it was all right, that I didn't mind. He said he didn't care if I didn't. There was another homeless man sitting with the shoe-shiner, watching us.

He started talking to me: "I've never seen him do this before."

"What?" I asked, squirming in my seat. I looked down at my shoes to see what havoc he was wreaking on the Spanish Cheveres that I bought at the Corte Ingles in Seville.

"I mean, I sit with this guy all the time, and this is the first shoe shine I've seen him do." I smiled. Calm returned. He was doing a fine job. The rain fell for a few more minutes, dampening my hair enough to mat it to my forehead. I let it hit my face and enjoyed the refreshing wetness on my skin.

As the drizzle ceased, I realized it had rained more than a few warm, late-summer drops. Mercy was falling that afternoon.

As the man was shining my shoes, my heart was moved. I noticed several looks of disdain from passersby, but the majority didn't pay attention. In fact, many looked the other way. These men weren't beggars. They weren't hitting people up for money. They were dirty and unkempt, but they wore smiles on their faces. They would say hello to businessmen and women as they passed by and get an occasional grunt of a reply, but that was about it. They were invisible people.

I gave my shoe-shiner more than the preplanned $1.50 in change in my pocket; in fact, I gave him most of what I had in my wallet. I wish I had given it all.

This was a breaking point. I was tired of choosing not to see what everyone else didn't see. I was tired of giving only what was reasonable. I was done with looking out for my own well-being. Done with being afraid. Done with thinking that my agenda is the most important one I will encounter today. I thanked the man and said a prayer of thanks for him, for God showing mercy on someone as poor in spirit as me through an unlikely figure.

He did a pretty good job shining my shoes, too.

FINDING CALCUTTA

Mother Teresa used to tell people wanting to join the Missionaries of Charity to stay home. She encouraged them to find their own "Calcutta," that they were everywhere. You just needed eyes to see it.

I didn't understand this until one day when I wandered down Gay Street in Nashville. I was walking the streets of a new city, thinking about a recent mission trip to Mexico I had taken months before. I had been hired recently by an international organization to tell missionaries' stories. But now that I was six months into the project, I was beginning to despair. What great story was *I* living?

There I was, longing to go overseas again—to experience the thrill of doing good in a foreign environment—when I saw Steve. Walking along the street, my friend Paul and I decided to stop and sit on a bench, with our backs facing the river and LP Field, the Tennessee Titans stadium.

Steve wandered in from across the street with a teeter to his walk and an awkwardness to his movements. After introducing ourselves, Paul gave him an apple, and he said thanks.

Steve was eager to talk, unlike the others we had met along the riverfront. We chatted about everything from the Chicago Cubs to Italian beef sandwiches to the importance of long underwear. It was winter, after all, and even in Nashville, things can get cold. He had had a bachelor's degree, a nice house in Indiana, and an unfortunate drug habit that brought him to Nashville for rehab. A year ago, his luggage, money, and ID were stolen as he was trying to check into a clinic, which drove him to the streets—the only place that would accept him.

This was his story, anyway, and despite my cynicism, I found myself believing it. When Steve spoke of his two sons, I saw an earnest desire in his eyes to provide for his boys, to do right by them. He longed to give his kids the best life possible, which was why he was staying away from home. However, he told me he planned on visiting them for Christmas.

I hadn't connected with someone so willing to share his story since that incident in Spain years ago.

Steve introduced us to the ways of homeless living. "If you do it right," he said with a wink, "you can eat a hot meal every night." We learned where to go and when in order to get the best food the city had to offer. All of this he said in a hushed tone, as if it was a secret. Maybe it was.

Paul asked Steve what he needed most, a question he

entertained for a moment. Then he shared something simple but essential: blankets. This led us to wonder where—and how—Steve and his companions slept. He started describing their sleeping situation when he stopped midsentence and said, "Wait—do you want to see it?"

Paul and I looked at each other, our eyes widening in both fear and excitement. We turned to our new, homeless friend and hesitantly nodded in agreement, unsure of where he was about to lead us.

After climbing over a waist-high, cement barricade that read "DEATH" in spray paint, the three of us navigated through over-grown shrubbery and down a worn path we almost slipped on a couple of times. We hiked down into a valley that formed the banks of the Cumberland River and, as we descended, the city gradually disappeared. Passing through the thick foliage of bushes and trees, we lost sight of businesses and bars and other buildings and were soon surrounded by another world.

And then we saw it.

Carved out of the concrete supporting the street on which we had just been standing was some kind of man-made cave, adorned with loose rocks and iron rebar. Inside was an encampment of six souls and all their possessions. As I stood there trying to take it all in, I looked up to where we had come from and realized something: we were now beneath the city. It wasn't the sewer. It was deeper than that. We were below Nashville.

Cans, bottles, and mud-caked clothes littered the camp. There were papers, blankets, and old shoes everywhere. I took a step and heard the crinkle of plastic bags and garbage underfoot, and I knew I was out of my element. Nearly a hundred feet above us was the city. Through the cracks in the foliage, I could see people passing by, but I was sure they couldn't see us. Even if they could,

I doubt they would have looked down. I know I never did. Never glanced over the guardrail, never peered through those bushes. I was too busy and in too much of a hurry to do that.

When I thought of homeless people living in Nashville, my imagination never conjured this. This camp. These lives. Ever since Spain, I had wanted to experience that same level of connection with someone as I had with Micah. When I finally got what I asked for, it stunned me. I always thought these people just aimlessly wandered the streets like vagrants. As it turns out, though, the homeless do have a home. I was looking at it, and it was hard for my eyes—and heart—to see. In a way, this sight was more disturbing than the idea that they slept on park benches and in alleyways.

Steve proudly showed us around and explained how he and his friends lived. As he did so, a couple of men returned to the camp. George and Jimbo. George didn't speak much English; nonetheless, the first word from his mouth when he met us was, "Jesus!" With wide eyes and rosy cheeks, he repeated it until Paul gave him a hug. "I think he just wanted to be touched," Paul later told me. I shook the surprisingly tender hand of George (whose name I think was really Jorge) and was warmed by the glow of his all-too-familiar smile, reminding me of one I had seen years ago in Seville.

Ten minutes later, we realized what we were doing. Reality began to settle in. We were in a camp below the street with a group of men who could do whatever they wanted to us and no one would ever know. Paul and I looked at each other, and with a nod of understanding said we ought to be going now, that we had something to get back to. Back to our world—back above. I wish I could say we weren't frightened, but we were. We knew what we were doing was risky.

Before we left, Steve explained there were countless other

communities like this one, camps along the river and hidden throughout the city—even groups of people that lived in caves. I couldn't believe it, and yet somehow, I could. After all, we had no idea this even existed.

We offered Steve a ride to his next hot meal, and he consented. When he entered my 1990 Buick Century, the small space filled with a stench that was hard to ignore and lingered after he had gone. When he left, I felt strangely compelled to sniff my hand that had just shaken his. I can't explain it, but I wanted this distinct scent to stay. Not because it was particularly pleasant, but because I didn't want to forget. I wanted to be reminded of a world which had been invisible to me only yesterday. I wanted to remember how much I had and how much I could help. Most of all, I wanted to be reminded that I, too, had a stench.

After meeting Steve, you could have told me a lot of things. You could have told me three-quarters of homeless people are mentally ill. You could've told me most are lazy or drunk—that the government does a good job of providing for them. But when you're staring poverty in the face—a dirty, lonely face—none of that matters. You just see someone with a need, a need you want to meet.

Every day, people like Steve don't know where their next meal is coming from. This kind of human need had been going on long before I ever took notice. And it will continue beneath the surface of the city, which ignorant people walk over every day of their lives. However, my encounter with a man who showed me the way was an introduction to a world I had no idea existed—one that would forever shape me.

At a distance, we see a need and ignore it. We judge it, condemn it, forget it. We don't think about it, because if we practice ignorance long enough, we don't notice the need anymore. It goes underground, and we're content with the surface of life as we know it—unwilling to break deeper ground. If all appears to be well on the outside, that is good enough for our consciences.

Mother Teresa was right—Calcutta is everywhere. I finally believed her. If we are willing to dig deep, to find Calcutta in our own backyards, we will find the poor. But we will also find God. And He may just open our eyes, so that we can see the need and not soon forget. So that we can hear their cries and not grow deaf. So that we can smell the stench of human need and awaken our hearts to compassion.

That's what happened to me. In Spain, I was changed. All because of one important choice: the choice to turn around. It didn't end there, of course. In Nashville, I continued to listen to that internal voice telling me to turn around. To take notice of the least and the left-out among us. And these kinds of actions began to shape how I lived my life every day.

Entering this underground world wasn't easy; in fact, it still isn't. But being aware of these needs I once ignored is important. Like all important lessons, I learned this through struggle. For me, my battle was with expectations. Everyone wanted me to do something amazing when I graduated college. My Spanish professors wanted me to go to graduate school in Europe. My writing professors wanted me to find a job with a magazine. But I didn't want to do any of that. I was ruined for an ordinary life, desperate for something more. And I found it in the most unlikely of places where no one else was willing to go: in the dumps and gutters and refuse centers of the world. There I found purpose. There I found Micah and Steve and countless others. I found peace and understanding of what it meant to live and be alive.

We all want this—to know what we're doing in this world has meaning and purpose. But so few are willing to pay the price to get it. These days, choosing discomfort looks more like doing the dishes or taking the dog for a walk. It takes the form of confronting a coworker or turning down an opportunity to travel to make sure a spreadsheet gets balanced. Still, the lesson is the same: the thing you try to avoid the most is often the remedy for your own self-centeredness. Once I grasped this, I gained deeper understanding of my calling—not any specific act itself, but the discomfort of doing the right thing in spite of how I feel.

On days when the email piles up and saving the world feels more like a mundane chore, I have to remember I didn't choose this work. It chose me. It shouted at me in broken English one night in Spain. And I haven't been able to tune it out since. Thank God.

CHAPTER 5

From Wrecked to
COMMITTED

"Sometimes, the hardest thing and the right thing are the same."
— THE FRAY

I believe in the importance of leaving home, of having an experience that wrecks you. There is something transformative that happens in a person's life when he leaves that which is comfortable for the first time. But there is also great value in sticking things out. If you've done the former but neglected the latter, then it may be time to make some longer-term commitments.

I am no good at commitment. It's the epic failure of my life. Calling my mom from a pay phone in Spain, I told her I wouldn't be home for Christmas. I did this, mind you, on Thanksgiving Day. She wasn't too pleased.

This noncommittal attitude followed me well into early adulthood. When I moved from Illinois to Tennessee, I got a part-time job and proposed to my girlfriend. Six months after living in a new city, I was ready to move on. I grew worried and anxious. Doubts assailed me: *What if this is the wrong choice? What if there is something else out there waiting for me? What then?*

Our culture is terrible about encouraging commitment. Everything around us is about ease and convenience. If you wait too long in line, give up. If your spouse upsets you, divorce her. Life is about you, after all, and what you want. Commit to the things that matter to you and when you stop caring, move on— that's our mentality.

The problem is that's not commitment. It's not much of a life, either.

There always is something more out there. Always something else to do, some great thrill to experience. Yet despite the challenge of forsaking all other possibilities and sticking with a plan, I've found there is great value to making commitments. Committing to certain things—a job, a wife, a calling—has taught me a lot about character and integrity, discipline and honor. There's something about the process of giving up on other possibilities and sticking to a path that brings life in ways that other thrills do not. And I'm a better man for it, no matter how much I kick and scream along the way.

C. S. Lewis called this the "quieter love."[18] It's what happens when the butterflies go away and all that's left is morning breath and annoying habits, replaced by a deeper appreciation and understanding. This is true for all things we love: work, play, relationships.

PRACTICING OUR CALLINGS

When I first started playing guitar, I hated it. I quit six times. I kept wanting to tear up the fret board like Jimmy Page. My dad (who was my teacher) would gently remind me, "You gotta learn to play a G chord first." I didn't want to hear that. I wanted the prestige of playing guitar without the pain of practicing.

I eventually stopped quitting and stuck with guitar. I got pretty good at it, too; I was even able to play a decent solo after a while. As soon as I graduated from college, I started touring with a band, playing shows nearly every day—something I did for about a year. I learned something important during those many months of touring. It's one thing to say you're going to do something; it's quite another to dedicate your life to the pursuit of it.

While we were touring, I got better at guitar than I ever thought possible. The weirdest part was I wasn't trying to be good. I had so many other responsibilities with the band that playing music felt like more of a job than a passion. But I didn't have a choice. I had to get up every day and play, whether I felt like it or not. As a result, without even intending to do so, I was practicing. So it is with all work we are all called to. When the passion goes away, it's the practice that sustains us.

This is the fruit of commitment, the reason it's worth the hardship. When you commit to something, anything, it allows you to practice what you love. And eventually, you get really good at it. Maybe even without noticing.

THREE LEVELS OF COMMITMENT

There are three levels of commitment we all must pass through in order to find our callings and live abundant lives. Commitment means something different at various life stages. As a child, you're committed to doing what your parents tell you, because they're your parents and that's what you're supposed to do. In high school and college, it's hard to commit to something that lasts longer than a semester. So much can change so quickly, it seems foolish to unnecessarily tether yourself to something so uncertain. As you enter adulthood, commitment takes on a different shape yet again. Through each season of life, we must relearn what it means to commit.

The first level of commitment is an adventure. In this season, you commit to something for the sheer thrill of it. This type of commitment marks those who travel the world and those who are able to walk away from a perfectly good job. Adventurers can move across the country or break up with a boyfriend without thinking twice. This type of commitment is important, because it helps you experience a broad array of opportunities life has to offer. It will lead you to see the world, explore different types of jobs, and do things you've never done before—as long as those things feel good. However, this is healthy only for a season.

When you build your entire life around this type of commitment, it can become a problem. You may find this way of living unfulfilling and immature as you grow and mature. I know I did. After spending a year of traveling from city to city and living in a van, I was fed up with wandering. I had seen so many homes and been a part of so many families, I was ready for something steady—if only for a season.

The second level of commitment is a season. You commit to something for an extended period of time, even after the initial thrill wanes. You plant seeds and stick around long enough to see them grow. You camp out at a job or under a revival tent, because there is something special about the place. You go through life with a certain group of people and get to know them pretty well. This is temporary. After the time of the commitment is complete, you move on to other endeavors. The season is over; the commitment is finished.

This is an important level of commitment that many people neglect. They jump from being completely reckless to starting a family—sometimes not on purpose. They go right from college to a full-time job and never feel like they had a chance to see what life had to offer. If you pursue seasonal commitments, you bridge the gap between adolescence and adulthood without getting bitter. As for length, a season is what you make it. Some last five months, while others last five years. My year on the road was a season, as was Dustin's two years in Guatemala. The point is that it serves a purpose (to teach you commitment) and has a definite end.

The third level of commitment is a marriage. This is the highest mark of maturity and what marks true dedication. Of course, it applies to more than actual matrimony, but you get the idea: marriage is forever, and so are some commitments. Hopefully, your calling fits under this category. Although jobs come and go, your vocation—your life's work—should be something that sticks. Something you can commit to. But how do you know it when you find it? You could do what my wife, Ashley, does. When she takes a job, she has a "marriage" mentality about it. She doesn't devise an exit strategy or consider her next steps. There are no stepping-stones in her book; she has no backup plans. Of course, she's open to promotion opportunities and other options that come along; she just doesn't plan on them. She's not like so many people her age, looking over her shoulder for something better to come along. She doesn't believe she will only have one job in her life; she just knows how always looking for the next best thing can sabotage your work and rob you of where you are now. Having a "marriage" mentality toward some commitments (although not all) is a healthy step to becoming a person of integrity.

ENTERING THE NEXT SEASON OF LIFE
The hardest part of going on an adventure is coming home. Frodo experienced this, along with his friend Samwise, in *The Lord of the Rings*. After being called on an adventure they didn't sign up for,

journeying from the safety of the Shire to the land of Mordor and destroying the ring of power, they eradicate all evil in the land—or so they think. The two travelers return to a land they once called home now decimated by the evil Lord Saruman. There is a mess for the heroes to clean up, which is where Sam comes in.

Most people believe the hero of the story is Frodo. He is, after all, the one who carries the ring and destroys it. But were it not for his faithful friend, he never would have succeeded. Sam is the one whose story we follow to the very end; he is the one who brings order to chaos. After Frodo sails away, Sam gets married, becomes mayor, and lives out the rest of his life in the Shire, bringing order and peace to the place where he grew up.

Here's the thing about adventures: they all have an ending. I'm willing to bet that the rest of Sam's life didn't look like it did on top of Mount Doom, where he and Frodo destroyed the ring. I bet he didn't encounter many fire-breathing monsters or axe-wielding dwarves (okay, maybe a few). I bet the rest of his life was pretty normal and that he was just fine with that.

This is the really hard part of getting wrecked—when the adventure ends. And it will. Even if you end up living in Africa, holding babies and living in mud huts, the adventurous feeling will eventually go away. Eventually, it'll feel just like a normal day at the office. And this is okay. Natural, even. This is how it's supposed to be.

We all have seen what happens when you don't go on some kind of epic adventure and get wrecked. We have seen people (maybe even parents or peers) experience midlife crises. They committed before getting wrecked, and it ruins them because they don't know what to do with the commitment. They spend the rest of their lives trying to relive their youth or recapture the dreams life stole from them. This is why commitment comes after the adventure, because you have to see the world is bigger than you—that it can break you—in order for you to focus on doing some good in it. That's what Samwise did, and it's what we must do, too. Being wrecked begins where the adventure ends.

At some point, you have to commit. Maybe it's a job or a marriage; maybe it's joining a church or buying a house. The point isn't what you do as much as it is that you do something to show you can stick around. If you've just had a time-of-your-life experience, this will sound like the last thing you want, but it's what you need.

NOT GOING IT ALONE

After meeting Steve and his community under the street in Nashville, I started going downtown about once a week. After months of these visits, I started to wonder if what I was doing was really making an impact. And one day I realized it wasn't.

I was visiting my homeless friends at a riverside park in downtown Nashville. I had built relationships with these people by serving them hotdogs every Saturday for lunch. We had known each other for months. We were friends. So when James came to me asking for some spare change, I didn't think anything of it. I pulled eighty-five cents out of my pocket, and he thanked me. He disappeared for about ten minutes. Then he returned—from the liquor store. My heart sank. James trotted back to his group of friends with a large bottle of malt liquor, nodding to me as he passed. He was beaming.

Great, I thought. *I just enabled a drunk.* That was it for me. I was fed up. Disappointed and frustrated, I packed up my stuff and decided to go home. Enough was enough. Here I was, having spent months trying to help these people. And it felt as if I had made no difference. No progress. So I decided to do something drastic. Something I dreaded doing. I decided to go to a shelter.

I didn't get involved in homeless ministry because I had some life-changing experience at a soup kitchen. Quite the opposite, actually. My heart broke when I met people on the street and liked them. As we became friends, I learned what they thought about life, people, and organizations that tried to help them. One common attitude was very clear: few people on the street trusted institutions like the Salvation Army or other local missions. My friends told me tales that shocked and horrified. As a result, I didn't like these institutions either. But I was at the end of my rope. What could I do? So I went to the mission to find out if what my friends told me was true. I was surprised by what I found. Clean beds. Delicious meals. A caring staff. Was this really the cutthroat den of danger and deception that my homeless friends described to me?

At first, I was skeptical. But after weeks of visiting and engaging with the people there, I saw more good happen—more impact and life change—than I had in six months on the street. I had to swallow my pride. I had to admit that I had pegged these guys all wrong. I couldn't serve the homeless on my own. I needed help. I needed a community—some brothers-in-arms to figure this out with.

I started serving every Tuesday at the mission. Every Tuesday for a year.

SERVING SOMEONE ELSE'S DREAM

Around the same time I began working at the mission, I started working for another nonprofit organization. I thought it was a short-term commitment, because everything I had done up to this point in life had lasted six to twelve months. It didn't take long, though, for me to realize I would be there longer than expected and that it would be years before I would be able to start thinking about my own dreams again. If I had known this going into the job, I wouldn't have taken it.

My first work project was to launch an online magazine telling missionaries' stories. This was followed by a short-term mission trip to Mexico, where I would be cataloguing stories of young people who were traveling the world. I was certain this fifteen-day trip would spark another season of adventure in me. I envisioned Machu Picchu. The Great Wall of China. Africa. All in the same year. This was going to be amazing. Maybe I would even write a book about it.

But I was rudely disappointed. Instead, all I got were spreadsheets, trips to Georgia (where our organization was based), and a new, shiny, $500 Dell laptop. Hardly the adventure I expected.

So what kept me there? It wasn't the paycheck (I had to raise my own salary). It was the opportunity to be part of something bigger than myself, to be led by vision and opportunity. Sure, I didn't get to participate in crazy, round-the-world journeys like I had in previous seasons of life, but I got something better: a chance to serve someone else's dream.

The concept of apprenticeship is largely lost in American culture today. These days, young adults don't have the opportunity, like previous generations had, to come under the leadership of a master craftsman. This is a foreign concept to most of us—at work, in our families, even at church. Instead, we offer lots of education with little application, followed by high expectation. No wonder we have a generation of Peter Pans, wandering through a series of short-term commitments and slow to grow up.

That first year of work, my job was hard. I was supposed to virtually "follow" (via email and the Internet) a group of fifty missionaries around the world and tell their stories. When I told people what I did, almost every person asked me, "Oh, that's great. Do you get to travel?"

"No," I would tell them, rolling my eyes. "I get to do something better. I get to write blog posts." I was only being half sarcastic. Part of me really enjoyed what I got to do. But part of me longed for an adventure. Selfishly, I wondered why I didn't get to be part of all the amazing experiences I was reporting on. Until one night I had a dream.

I dreamed I finally got to go. I visited one of our teams in Africa, and my boss, Seth, was there. I showed up unexpectedly, hoping to be greeted with smiles and high fives. Instead I received strange looks, and Seth said, "Jeff, what are you *doing*? You shouldn't be here." I frowned, but shrugged off the discouragement. I went around to the different groups telling them how I was there to join them in the work they were doing. But each group I approached received me in the same way: "What are you doing here? You're not supposed to be here!" So I turned around and headed home. Apparently I had a different role to serve. I woke up sweating. Five years later, the dream still lingers.

Since then I've gotten to travel some, but my life most days is filled with phone calls, email, and meetings. From the outsider's perspective, it looks normal. But for me, it's one of the most fulfilling things I could do in this season. I do it for a few reasons. One, I've learned that an adventure is not an end to itself but a means to something bigger. Two, when work feels mundane (because it probably is), I remind myself that I am disciplining myself—learning to put off short-term gratification for long-term joy.

In serving my boss and submitting to his leadership (which I trust), I get to see firsthand what a dream realized looks like. I get to understand the complexities of running an organization, leading hundreds of staff, and still keeping your heart and soul grounded in what matters most. Sometimes, it's a discipline, but most of the time, it feels like a gift. And I consider it preparation for what's to come.

My friend Alece Ronzino knows the power of commitment; she's lived it like few have. She helps nonprofits tell their stories, but she didn't always do that. For over a decade, she lived as a missionary in Africa, working with a ministry called Thrive Africa that she started. All of this began with a trip to rural Botswana when she was fifteen. The two months she spent there changed her life. Here's what happened in her own words:

> This city girl from Long Island who would rather spend a gorgeous day indoors than outdoors spent her summer in a tent, cooking over a campfire, and only showering every ten days—and absolutely loved it! My heart was captivated by the beautiful people of southern Africa, and I knew I wanted to return long-term. That summer was a pivotal time that literally changed the entire trajectory of my life. God wrecked my heart for missions, for Africa, and for living fully surrendered to Him.

Sounds typical, right? Kid goes on a short-term mission trip, feels guilty for having so much privilege, and promises to make a difference. Thousands of American teenagers and young adults do it every year. But what happened next was anything but ordinary. Alece did what few of us do: she decided to go back. She decided to do the hard work of committing to a cause and paying the cost to actually see it through. Here's how she described what happened after she came back from that first trip:

> When I got off the plane from that first mission trip to Africa, I told my parents, "I'm going back!" I returned the following summer, and after graduating high school, I participated in a yearlong internship serving at the missions organization I'd traveled overseas with. While I was there, I helped them set up their

first ever mission trip to South Africa and then helped lead that inaugural team the following summer. That trip cemented in my heart the dream and desire to return to southern Africa long-term. I finished my internship, returned home to New York to fund-raise, and then, armed with only two overflowing suitcases and a heart filled with probably more foolishness and naiveté than faith, I headed out to South Africa.

Alece was nineteen years old. And for the next decade, she served as a missionary in Africa, helping empower local leaders to make a difference in their own communities. She is an inspiration and challenge to so many young people who want to make their lives matter. This is the cost: doing what she did by giving her life away.

Alece was wrecked by her first visit to Africa, but it was in the staying that the transformation took place. Change always happens when you come down from the clouds and deal with the messiness of life. When you turn a mission trip into a lifestyle. When you walk past someone who is poor and in pain and actually turn around. Real transformation happens when you commit.

Every time I lead a mission trip, I hear the same vows from teenagers (and sometimes adult sponsors, too): "We're going to come back next year!" "We're going to adopt this community!" "We're going to pray for you every day!" Those are all great promises, but they aren't decisions. You can't make a decision on the airplane—up in the air where cabin pressure is low and you're not thinking practically. Real decisions are made the way Alece made hers. They're made when you step off the plane.

PERSEVERING THROUGH THE DIPS OF CONFLICT

The highest form of commitment is the rarest. Because it costs so much: your pride, time, and resources. Frankly, some relationships and jobs aren't worth it. Often it's best to move on and find something or someone worth your time. But in really special cases, what you need to do is persevere.

Our culture is so self-oriented and consumer-driven, we probably need to correct our tendency toward flakiness with defaulting to more of a committed posture when we approach work and relationships. I have seen this best exemplified by some of my closest friends. When it was easiest to move on, to discard the friendship due to inconvenience, we instead decided to stick with it. My friend Dustin and I have a habit of doing this. We have been friends since my freshmen year of college and seen each other at our best and worst. We've traveled through Europe and road-tripped to Texas together; we were best men at one another's weddings. Every few years, when it feels like our friendship is going stale, one of us does something to revive it.

Three months after getting married and starting their new lives in Oklahoma, Dustin and his wife, Kristen, drove eleven hours to Nashville for a surprise weekend visit to celebrate my birthday. It wasn't easy or cheap, but it spoke volumes to me. This is the hard part of friendship, the not-so-fluffy stuff that's easy to ignore. But it's what makes the mundane parts of life worth living. It's an unexpected thank-you note. A favor. A surprise date. An otherwise unnecessary blessing done anyway. In a word, it's grace.

Commitment is hard. I'll admit that for me, it can sometimes be a pain. In fact, I think it's supposed to be. If a fulfilled life is about not avoiding the hard parts of a suffering world, then that includes the pain of pressing into the difficulty of sticking through the messiness of everyday, ordinary relationships we'd otherwise ignore. This is where the good stuff is found, where we find the joy of being understood by people who have sacrificed for us in incredible ways. But we don't know this pleasure if we keep bouncing from one thing to the next, if we never commit. If not for your own sake, do it for the person on the other end—the one who's waiting for you to drive halfway across the country just to show you care.

You need commitment in order to grow. It's just that simple. It begins with a season—something like joining a church or choosing a certain educational track. Then stick with it for longer than you'd like. Regulate the urge to leave and tell yourself that it will be worth it in the long run, and it will be. When it gets tough, don't allow yourself to quit (unless it's unhealthy for you to stay). As a result, you grow—maybe like never before.

CHAPTER 6

The Fruit of
COMMITMENT

"It's better to be in the arena, getting stomped by the bull, than to be up in the stands or out in the parking lot."

— STEVEN PRESSFIELD

Once you've tasted a life that isn't all about you, it can wreck you. It runs so contrary to our "me first" culture that it can turn your world upside down. Those who have experienced it can't help but feel like misfits. They are unsatisfied with the way things are. They want to experience a life that's meaningful. They're restless. They've been wrecked and can't look back. On one level this is healthy and helpful; on another, it's distracting and missing the point. Ultimately, restlessness is not enough.

An unchecked dissatisfaction with the status quo will lead to a reckless lifestyle of bouncing from one thrill-seeking adventure to the next with little commitment to place or person. I've seen this happen a lot, and it breaks my heart, because your life is about more than your next adventure. That's not to say you have to live some kind of cloistered life; quite the opposite, in fact. What it does mean is that in order to really be wrecked, you've got to commit. And as you do so, you'll unlock the secrets to some of life's greatest mysteries—like how to be happy, for example.

The other day, I was at a coffee shop and overheard two people in their early twenties talking. One was a girl who was apparently visiting from out of town. She had recently gone on some kind of mission trip and couldn't stop talking about it. The other was a guy she was trying to convince to do the same. At first, I agreed with her. But then the conversation took a turn.

> COMMITMENTS HELP US BECOME BETTER PEOPLE.

"I should be engaged, you know," she said. "We looked at a ring and everything. It would've happened," she paused for dramatic effect to let the young man know she was serious. Then she continued, "Well, if I didn't leave." For thirty minutes, they shared stories, talking about the things they had given up—all for God, they claimed.

Those are powerful words: *If I didn't leave.* As they continued dialoguing, I was struck with a sober realization. As someone who works for a short-term missions organization, I'm a proponent of these types of experiences. But what I was hearing was disturbing, because the point of a trip is to lead you to a destination. And these two people just seemed to be aimlessly wandering. The young woman's experience overseas had fueled her restlessness, setting her on a series of adventures and voyages that didn't seem to be leading anywhere. I had to wonder if all this traveling was actually helping her find purpose or merely feeding her restlessness. Which, of course, is not the point.

This is not what God has for us—bouncing from one spiritual experience to another, ditching one part-time job for the next, starting intimate relationships and then abandoning them after a few months of "trying things out." That's not to say we should commit to the first steady opportunity that comes along without asking deeper questions about life. Yes, in this age of opportunity we have unlimited freedom to try out different experiences, but the whole point of the search is to actually find something. If we don't, then we're more lost than when our journeys began.

God wants to use our restlessness to call us out of the world and into a new reality characterized by order, not chaos. The point of our wandering is to eventually end up in the Promised Land. This is where most young people go wrong. They chase experiences and events and fail the test of commitment. In so doing, they miss out on one of life's greatest gifts. It's time to change that.

COMMITTING TO NOTHING

The late Chuck Colson (who at one point was an adviser to President Nixon) wrote an article for *Christianity Today* in 2010 in which he lamented Generation Y's lack of commitment. He cited studies revealing how twentysomethings struggle these days to commit to anything: careers, marriages, even their faith.

As a man in his eighties, Colson said, "My single greatest joy is giving myself to others and seeing them grow in return. You cannot discover that without commitment." In 2008, according to the article, half of American employees between ages 20 and 24 had been with their current employer for less than a year. Colson continues:

> By abandoning commitment, our narcissistic culture has lost the one thing it desperately seeks: happiness. Without commitment, our individual lives will be barren and sterile. Without commitment, our lives will lack meaning and purpose. After all, if nothing is worth dying for (the anthem of the '60s anti-war

protesters), then nothing is worth living for. But with commitment comes the flourishing of society—of calling, of marriage, of the church—and of our hearts. It's the paradox Jesus so often shared when he bid us to come and die that we might truly live.[19]

We cannot live our best lives if we continue living like prodigal children, wandering aimlessly with little consistency or focus. We will leave no legacy and have no impact if we do not learn this lost art of commitment.

We make excuses for avoiding commitment. My Christian friends often couch their reasons for not committing in spiritual justifications. They want to be open to what God might have for them, or they haven't received "confirmation" through prayer. Whatever the reason, they just don't move. My friends who aren't Christians say they're "following their hearts." Both are saying the same thing: they're afraid to decide. If they commit to something, their reasoning runs, that would inhibit them from being able to pursue other opportunities. So they wait. Instead of taking a full-time job or signing an apartment lease, they work part-time at Starbucks and live in their parents' basement. They're not really waiting; they're stalling. They are delaying the pain of making a decision and living with the consequences. So they hesitate and weigh the options—all the while, completely unaware of the cost.

There is profound spiritual value in making commitments. By moving to a more committed lifestyle, you learn how to be a friend, meet a deadline, follow through on a task, and push through a challenge. Commitments help us become better people.

There are milestones in life that we only reach by making a tough choice, one that involves forsaking all other options. Like how to really love someone or the beauty of a long-term relationship—these are the lessons we need to learn. And the way we learn them is through commitment.

I want to be the kind of person who doesn't stall, who faces a decision and boldly steps into it, aware of all the other opportunities I'm missing. I don't want to be afraid of what I'm missing; instead, I want to embrace what I get to experience. I have a long way to go, but I'm getting there, one commitment at a time. I want that for my friends, too.

EXTENDED ADOLESCENCE

There are other reasons for our instinct to avoid commitment. It's what's expected of us. Inexplicably, society tolerates a lack of integrity, especially among people in their twenties who are still "figuring things out." This is due to a cultural acceptance of extended adolescence, a fascinating topic worth Googling sometime. In short, we have lowered our expectations of young people, and they have, in effect, "lived down" to those expectations.

In his book *Teen 2.0*, Robert Epstein explains that the phenomenon of adolescence was catalyzed by the Industrial Revolution. The introduction of child labor laws led to young people's primary place being in the educational system, which led to the creation of youth culture. Soon, this unique culture attracted music, art, and commerce to support it. In fact, if you look around today, you can still see the effects of it. Many middle-aged parents dress like their teenage children, and it's becoming more accepted for people well into their adult years to not know what to do with their lives.

In 1991, a study of 186 countries revealed that more than a hundred didn't even have a word for adolescence. "Where teen problems are beginning to emerge in various countries around the world," Epstein writes, "they can be traced to the increasing isolation of teens from adults brought about by Western educational practices, labor restrictions and media."[20]

If you've ever traveled to another country, especially in the developing world, you may have noticed that you don't see many moody teenagers. Young adults in the rest of the world aren't like they are in America. Other cultures make a clear delineation between childhood and adulthood; there are rites of passages and initiation ceremonies to mark these transitions. People expect and are willing to expose young people to hardship and pain, because it helps them grow. There is apprenticeship and a cultural precedent for strong family bonds. Where this isn't the case, it's usually due to the influence of Western culture, primarily through music, movies, and television. In other words, adolescence is a modern, and particularly Western, phenomenon.

Somehow, in all of our advancement and technology, we've lost the sacredness of family and tribal connections—the very relationships that help people grow into who they're made to be. In exchange for these things, we have a unique youth culture, low expectations of what young people are capable of, and a lot of education. We have more legal restrictions for what young people can and can't do, and there is still a blurred line between adulthood and childhood. And don't forget: we have more entertainment tools than ever. Doesn't quite seem worth the trade-off, does it?

We need to break this cycle of extended adolescence. We need to help young people transition well into adulthood. Perhaps we need to grow up ourselves. We need to, in a sense, look backward, not forward. What have societies around the world always done to mark the emergence into adulthood? What are other cultures still doing that we're not? That's what we need to be doing.

We need initiation—the older generation walking with the younger one, helping them learn where to walk and how. This is called mentorship, and it's grossly needed in our schools, churches, and culture. I meet a lot of young people who understand this, but don't take the initiative to find someone to guide them. Which raises an important point: it's not the mentor's responsibility to begin mentoring; it's the student's. We need practical training where young people, even children, learn by doing, not merely watching or hearing.

We don't give young people enough credit. If challenged, they will rise to the occasion. The world is full of remarkable young people just like Zach Hunter, waiting for their chance to step up and do something. While many of his peers are chasing girls and mastering Angry Birds, Zach has been fighting human trafficking. Since he was twelve, he has been raising money, writing books, and speaking to youth about ending modern-day slavery.[21] Why is it that Zach is changing the world, while plenty of thirty-year-olds still haven't moved out of their mom's attic? The answer is adolescence.

Belonging to a ministry that works with teens and young adults, I found this phenomenon to be fascinating and relevant to what we do. It rang true for me, because I've seen it. I've seen people travel the world and then return home unable to make a simple decision. I've seen middle schoolers ready to be empowered and eager to demonstrate their talents. I've seen kids defy the expectations of their parents, youth leaders, and even themselves. The reason we don't see more of this, I believe, is because we refuse to let young people fail.

This happened to me when I got my first "real" job at twenty-three. I had just finished a yearlong commitment with a traveling music ministry, but this was my first legitimate employment opportunity as a college grad. I was hired as a staff writer and quickly became the marketing director, a leader in the organization. Since I was young and inexperienced, I sometimes ran into people who weren't sure how to treat me. As I worked alongside people who were twice my age—and we were peers—they would sometimes question my judgment or ability. Quite frankly, I didn't blame them. But something subtle was sabotaging me here; it was the thought that I wasn't good enough, that I didn't have what it took to do the job, despite the fact that my boss clearly believed in me.

I've seen this self-doubt manifested in others, too. It's a common story: some young leader becomes empowered and doesn't know what to do with his newfound authority and suddenly rebels. In an accusatory tone, he'll question the judgment of his superior, saying, "What do you mean you want me to do this? I'm not ready!" All the while, what he's really saying is this: *I don't believe in myself, so why do you?*

I know people think these things, because I thought them. When I was twenty-two, I was asked to lead a team of musicians around the country for a year. When the road manager asked me out to lunch and told me he wanted me to be a leader, I almost quit. I felt scared and unprepared. Why couldn't someone else do it? But there was no one else, and that much was clear. I took the job, even though I didn't feel qualified. Although I failed and got frustrated many times, I survived, which was a miracle in itself. My team followed me even through tough times, and we came out the other end alive. In the process, I learned an important lesson: I could do things I didn't think I could do. As life went on, I realized this is a crucial tenet to living a wrecked life: learning confidence in the face of insecurity and inadequacy.

If you feel you've been given more than you can possibly handle, take heart. This is the point where you learn to grow into who you're meant to be. It's when you're in over your head that you start taking your work seriously, when you finally grow up and into your destiny.

No one's going to give you a map. You must make your own way.

GETTING OVER YOUR COMMITMENT PHOBIA

There's something spiritual to the discipline of commitment. Something shared in the simple transaction of a handshake or a spoken agreement. The Bible is full of these encounters. God makes promises with men and women, and people make promises with each other and even with God. These promises are called covenants, and they run deeper and last longer than our fickle desires. In an age of instant gratification, we must once again become people of covenant.

Many people haven't discovered the hidden blessing of commitment. Of course, it's hard to be an adult—to pay bills, work forty hours a week, go to bed early, and so on. I struggle with these things myself. But little by little, I'm learning the value of being forced to show up on time, come through for people, and stick around long enough to see real change happen. Marriage has certainly taught me this, but so has work and ministry.

When my wife and I were newly married, it was a challenge for me to adjust to someone else's schedule. Since I worked out of my home, I was used to getting up around ten o'clock in the morning, taking a couple hours for lunch, and then finishing around eight at night. So it was a rude awakening when my wife came home at 5:30 and expected me to spend the rest of the evening with her. We spent months arguing about this, but finally I realized that if I wanted to see my bride, I was going to have to adjust my schedule. It wasn't comfortable, but it was the right thing to do.

Any semblance of maturity I have (which isn't much) has come about through some sort of struggle. Some hard talk or difficult circumstance that forced me to see my own selfishness and grow up a little. The only thing that's allowed me to see victory on the other side has been a choice to commit. To stick it out when times got tough. What you ought to be looking for in your search for your life's calling is struggle, not resolution. When I meet people who show no signs of struggle or hardship or pain, I usually find an adolescent in an adult's body.

Think of people you know who have lived a full, abundant life. What do they tell you? What wisdom do you glean? Typically they talk about the hard times, the difficulties they faced and how they overcame them. You hear how they resolved to do something regardless of the opposition, and then did it. You hear about commitment and perseverance.

In anything worth doing, there is a necessary downside. In order to experience ultimate satisfaction, you must embrace the hard things. You must commit. The alternative is to avoid pain and shirk responsibility. But if you do that, you will be costing yourself the fruit that only comes with showing up and sticking around. The ease is hardly worth the sacrifice.

Struggle shapes our character. And character dictates what we will become. Commitment is a necessary part of becoming all that God has intended. For the average person, such a challenge sounds daunting—scary, even. What can we do? We must risk.

Any commitment is a risk. That's a given. However, we need to consider the greater risk of waiting. Waiting for the right person. The perfect job or opportunity. Waiting because we're scared to decide. Every leader I know and aspire to be like knows something that I, an undisciplined twentysomething, do not: greatness doesn't come cheap. I think of my boss who finally won over his wife after chasing her for years, writing her poems while she was engaged to another man. When all seemed to have been lost, she finally came around, and he rose the victor. I think of a friend who regularly gives five-figure financial gifts to individuals and charities without their knowing. I think of my parents who divorced and then remarried one another to give each other and their children the best life they could.

Every great sports film tells the tale of an average Joe who pushes through and perseveres when others are slacking off. While one grows complacent in his accomplishments, the hero is working hard, getting stronger. These heroic stories and epic tales are all preaching the same gospel: greatness has a cost. We know this; yet, so few of us are willing to walk through the mire, to spend countless hours doing the hard, thankless work of heroes. Not for the satisfaction of today, but tomorrow. We are unwilling to rise to the occasion because we're too scared or maybe too scatterbrained to stick with the process for the long haul. Yes, greatness has a cost, and its name is commitment.

According to blogger Seth Godin, what sets difference-makers apart from the rest of the pack is patience. He writes, "I discovered a lucky secret the hard way about thirty years ago: you can outlast the other guys if you try. If you stick at stuff that bores them, it accrues. Drip, drip, drip you win."[22] I'm a bit impatient myself, but I'm learning to do something I never thought I could do: commit. In the end, it's worth it. And it's the only way greatness is achieved.

You can't achieve success without pledging yourself to something. You can't take a relationship to the next level without making a choice. Sure, it costs you something; it probably costs you a hundred somethings. Every choice to do one thing means a choice to not do something else. But it also costs you the anxiety of waiting, freeing you from the trap of decision paralysis. Committing to a cause sets you free.

When I joined the workforce, I had in my mind the picture

of a perfect job. When my experience didn't meet that ideal, I got scared and wanted to leave. I regularly thought of quitting, of finding something else that would hopefully fit the picture I had conjured in my head. For some reason, though, I didn't quit. Something wouldn't let me. I think it was knowing that what was hard was also right. So I stayed for one year. And then another and another still. Slowly, I hung around while I saw others come and leave, often chasing the promise of something better, but rarely finding it. As I watched people come and go, I grew grateful for the fact that I had stayed. I was seeing something few people had the privilege of seeing: I was watching myself grow.

The fact that we fear commitment is what makes it so great. Some blessings only come with long-term investment. They may be less grand than the quick and erratic changes that mark adolescence, but they are far better in the long haul. When we work past our phobia and commit to something, we find a deeper, lasting joy. It may be subtle at first, but it's far more beautiful than the temporary thrills we are so often tempted with.

Some assignments in life require more than a season to come to fruition. Certain forms of greatness take time. They require blood, sweat, and tears before you see the harvest. This could be a job, a class, or a relationship, but we all eventually face a decision that requires something that costs us dearly. We want to hold back, to minimize our losses. So we play it safe, which is stupid. Because this is precisely where we grow—when we have to. It's important to not shy away from these opportunities.

When you come across these situations where you feel uncomfortable, don't hesitate. This is war. Something is holding you back; don't let it. Don't wait for more information if it's not going to come. Don't "sleep on it." Don't procrastinate. These are all distractions—subtle forms of deception, defeating countless leaders that could be making a difference right now. Embrace the challenge. Make the choice. Commit and do something. The fruit is always worth the pain.

OUR OBSESSION WITH "NEW"

Sometimes what holds us back from making committed decisions is the excitement of doing something new. We like "new." I once heard a public speaker explain that "new" is always attractive, that we should always be looking for ways to portray what we're doing as new. Newness is attractive, but this obsession with constant innovation can be dangerous. We humans tend to be capricious, and chasing after the shiniest new toy isn't always the right thing to do.

Personally, I like old stuff. I prefer a used, hardbound book to a brand-new, glossy paperback or Kindle. I like food that takes a long time to prepare. I enjoy wearing clothes from Goodwill. I've always been this way. As a teenager, I listened to classic rock music—bands like Led Zeppelin and Pink Floyd. Now, I'm drawn to obscure blues and local jazz artists and often sport a pocket watch my wife gave me for our anniversary. Sometimes when I'm in the car by myself, I turn on the classical music station or listen to talk radio. Yes, I'm turning into a senior citizen, and I wouldn't change it for the world.

Some friends say I have an "old soul," which is fine with me. I don't want to have a new soul, not if it means abdicating to our modern obsessions with bigger, faster, and better. I want to give my spirit room to breathe and reflect in this overcrowded world. I want to go for long walks and watch black-and-white movies. I want to dance with my wife to a big band, not a DJ. When we attend a concert, I want to sit down with a drink and a snack and not have my ears bleed. I want to carry a money clip wherever I go.

We need more of the old and less of the new. There is something about taking your time in doing something that makes it more worthwhile, isn't there? Something beautiful about the old ways of doing things—I am sure of it. And this, of course, includes how people used to make choices: by letting their *yes* mean yes and their *no* mean no. In an age when nearly anything can be mass produced, we need to be careful with this obsession with novelty. We may find ourselves losing the old things that are most important to our humanity—things like doing what we say and honoring our commitments. As the prophet Jeremiah warned: "Stand at the crossroads and look; ask for the ancient paths, ask where the good way is, and walk in it, and you will find rest for your souls. But you said, 'We will not walk in it.'"[23] We need to find an old way today, and walk in it.

A NEW (OLD) STANDARD

We need a new standard for young people. Clearly, the impression we're giving the world is not a good one. I want to leave a lasting legacy in the world, and right now, I haven't done a great job at that. I've not come through on promises I've made, not showed up when I said I would, and blown off obligations. But I'm trying now to remedy the havoc I've caused with my immaturity, because I realize I won't get a second chance at life. I only get one shot, and I don't want to blow it. I know others who are setting similar goals for themselves—people who realize that time is short and the difference they want to make in the world is tied closely to their character. Our crippling fear of commitment is killing us. Fortunately, there is an alternative to flaking out—one that satisfies the fleeting passions of adolescence without forcing you to lock into a lifelong obligation: develop the discipline of seasonal commitments.

It's okay to treat your twenties like a series of internships, but instead of changing your lifestyle every six to twelve months, try adopting a new standard: a minimum two-year commitment to anything you're serious about doing. A lot of people I know skip out on a commitment once it gets hard. This is not just twenty-somethings, but people in their thirties, forties, and fifties. They never learned how to stick with something. As a result, their life is a series of short-term commitments that don't add up to much. The unfortunate byproduct of this lifestyle is if you don't commit to something soon, you may never do so. If you don't acquire the discipline to push through a personal low point, you will miss the reward that comes with persevering.

At the same time, it's unrealistic to expect people still finding their way in the world to jump right into a commitment and stick with it for decades. There needs to be a way for twentysomethings to acquire legitimate life skills while experiencing the freedom of moving around and trying out different things. There is. It's called a seasonal commitment.

A seasonal commitment can mean a lot of things. It may be sticking with a job for another year when you'd rather walk out the door tomorrow. It may mean giving that relationship another shot or deciding to renew your lease when restlessness seems to be calling you away. According to Barna Group president David Kinnaman, young people often leave their jobs too soon. When you feel you're at your breaking point, he says you should stay longer. "Sticking it out in a job that is a struggle may be the best thing for your character," Kinnaman writes. "Maybe the company or the situation is bad. But what if your future will be even more difficult? What if God is getting you ready for an even tougher assignment?"[24] Maybe it means dealing with your restlessness in other ways than just permanently skipping town. A group of men

I know go on biannual hikes in the mountains to rediscover their ruggedness and give restlessness an outlet.

My friend Josh, who moved cross-country to Portland from Atlanta and then to Austin with his wife, recently admitted it's hard to stay put in a place when restlessness kicks in. However, he knows how to control his restlessness better than most. He won't commit to something for less than two years. Even when life was hard in Oregon and he felt the call to leave, he and his wife took their time deciding. They valued the relationships they had built and were worried about constantly chasing the next exciting opportunity. Josh wanted to build trust with the people in his life, and he knew that only comes with time and intentionality. So he stayed put until he was absolutely sure he should go. Doing so caused him to learn a lot about community, choices, and commitment. When tempted to leave, we would do well to follow Josh's example by sticking through something even when it gets uncomfortable until we are absolutely sure it's time to move on. Looking back, we may realize how much we learned.

CHAPTER 7

When You Have
to Walk AWAY

"Somewhere we know that without silence words lose their meaning, that without listening speaking no longer heals, that without distance closeness cannot cure."

— HENRI NOUWEN

The worst part of being wrecked is facing a need and then having to walk away. It happens, even when we don't want it to. Especially then. For one reason or another, we must sometimes pass the baton on to the next person God is calling to heal a wound. We must let go; we must leave what is comfortable and familiar and once again trust. Sometimes people leave our lives of their own volition; other times, they are violently torn from our arms, and we wonder why. Sometimes God doesn't "close a door and open a window." Occasionally He slams the door on your fingers, and you're left with a throbbing pain, unsure of where you went wrong. At least, that was my experience, and I'm still trying to make sense of it.

"LET IT GO"

It was October, and I was volunteering with an organization in Nashville that delivers groceries to people's homes. This is a service for people who don't have transportation, are physically disabled, or just aren't able to get out to go shopping. They usually don't have the money to buy groceries, either.

I met a single mother named Michelle on a delivery run. She was pregnant. Besides her two kids, Michelle was alone. She lived in a small duplex that she rented between two large public housing projects. After meeting her family, I felt a connection to all three of them. In fact, the experience kind of haunted me.

When we first delivered groceries to Michelle's house, she couldn't stop crying. She was so grateful. When my friend Bruce and I offered to put away the bags and boxes of dry goods in her kitchen, she said, "No, leave them. I want the kids to see when they wake up." So we left them in her living room. On the floor. When we offered to pray for her, she cried again.

I couldn't get Michelle's sobs out of my head. For days afterwards, I woke up in the middle of the night thinking about her and her family, wondering how they were doing. So I went back and visited. They welcomed me in their home with open arms. So I made it a regular thing. About every week or so, I would drop by. Sometimes I would watch a movie with the kids; other times, I'd bring cookies. In some weird way, we became family.

In December, I knocked on Michelle's door. With me was a tall, artificial Christmas tree in a long brown box. Michelle was blown away when she saw the tree. She had told me that the one thing she wanted more than anything that year was for her kids to have Christmas.

Two weeks later, I pulled up to her house with a car full of presents. I told her this wasn't me or my friends from church or any other person that was providing for her. It was God. It felt good to bring tangible hope into a person's life—a little too good. Whenever Michelle would express gratitude for what we were doing, I would quickly correct her, informing her that God was the one who was providing and that she could trust in that.

A week after dropping off the Christmas presents, some friends and I took Michelle's kids to the zoo and then out for dinner at McDonald's. More than anything, I noticed that the kids just wanted to be touched. I even got to hold the little boy's hand when he was acting tough. At the end of the day, we dropped them off at their mom's. She was tired but grateful. We said good-bye and told them we loved them.

And that was the last time we ever saw them.

My wife, Ashley, and I were married that January. We had a wonderful honeymoon. After returning home, I said, "We should go visit Michelle." But life got busy. We were adjusting to our new life together, sharing a home (and bathroom), and growing in all the ways that young married couples do. We trusted Michelle was doing well, though her due date was quickly coming. To my surprise, a month went by without our even realizing it.

The pressures of work, marriage, and building a new life consumed us.

One day, I thought about Michelle and decided we needed to visit her and the kids soon. We talked about it for another two weeks before it actually happened. Ashley baked some cookies, and we drove over to their house after church one Sunday to drop them off. We knocked and knocked, but no one answered the door. We looked around, shrugged, and left, and spent the afternoon at the mall.

Two weeks later, my friend Joel and I dropped by to see Michelle. We got out of the car, walked up to the door, and knocked. No answer. There were a bunch of envelopes stuffed into the mailbox. I knocked again. A white man (who was out of place in that neighborhood) stopped us and asked, "Can I help you?"

"No, thanks," I said. "We're fine." I continued to knock on the door to no avail. I wished this man would mind his own business.

"Well, I own this building," he replied. Instantly, I remembered all the cruel things Michelle had told me about this man—how he had turned off the heat on her family, how they had to use the oven to stay warm some nights, how he kept charging more for rent and had zero sensitivity to their situation. "No one has lived here for two months," he told me.

My heart sank, and I started to feel sick.

The landlord said he knew Michelle. He told me she just up and left one day—maybe two, three months ago. I couldn't believe it. I knew she was unhappy, but she had always said she planned to stay until the summer to finish out her lease. I was scared. It was now March, and Michelle was due to go into labor soon. The landlord told us she may have moved in with her mother who lived down the street.

Joel and I proceeded to knock on every door. It was useless. No one answered. I stood in the street, my head hung low. I wondered why this happened. I asked God why He would let it. Didn't He see the good we were doing in this family? Had I been lazy or negligent? Was this my fault?

Then I remembered the voice.

Back in January, I heard something that might have given me a clue that all this would happen. I might've been able to prepare. My wife and I were at the mall, and I was sitting on a bench, waiting for her to exit a store. This was a voice I had ignored, a voice that was now ringing in my head as I stood outside of Michelle's old home, wondering what had happened.

Let it go, the voice said.

I don't know what you believe about prayer and miracles and such, but I'm pretty much a skeptic about the Creator speaking to me through audible voices and oddly shaped pancakes. But every once in a while, something happens to me that is unarguably God. This was one of those moments.

This was not the first time I had heard the phrase. It had popped into my mind one afternoon in December, too. I was praying for Michelle, and I heard those words in my mind as clear as day: *Let it go, Jeff.*

I thought, *Are you serious?* My mind must have been playing tricks on me. I shared the thought with a friend, and she thought it sounded absurd that God would be telling me to let go of a relationship. A few weeks later, I prayed and seemed to hear the same thing. I didn't believe it.

As I was standing at Michelle's door, listening to her landlord tell me this friend of mine had taken off very close to the same time I heard those words in my mind, I started to wonder. Maybe this wasn't just a random thought that popped into my head. Maybe God was proving what I had always told Michelle—that He was her provider, not me. And maybe He was still providing for her right now. Maybe God didn't need me.

I still struggle with feeling like we abandoned Michelle, like maybe I could have done more. But that's not really productive. I know that I'd do some things differently if I had the chance to do them again. But I also know that this is an important lesson to learn for anyone who does work that requires compassion: sometimes, you have to walk away.

In visiting Michelle and doing other things, I had grown codependent, getting my self-worth from what I did for others in need. I shared this story of Michelle with a friend of mine who passed it on to his family that evening. Over dinner, he retold the story, and his young daughter responded, "Daddy, do you think God made that woman move so that someone besides Jeff could have a chance to bless her?" He only smiled and nodded. I must learn to do the same.

I don't know what happened to Michelle. I never got to run into her at the grocery store to see her smiling face. I never got to see the story resolved. It will always be a painful memory. But in that pain, I'm learning to trust. Maybe these scars serve as reminders to me to be more intentional, to have more faith, and to learn that I'm not ultimately in control. I can only hope.

LOSING YOUR SOUL TO SAVE THE WORLD

This is not easy, this letting go. There is so much need and so much pain—so much suffering—that it seems self-centered to walk away from a need. But this isn't about the need; it's about humility. It's about believing that there is more happening than we can see when we bring a cool cup of water to someone who is thirsty. It's about having faith in a deeper narrative that underlies every compassionate act.

In other words, it's easy to lose yourself in the pursuit of justice.

Nobody wants to tell you this. That this may cost you your soul. That it will hurt worse than you imagined and there will be all kinds of unresolved tensions. You never see a disclaimer at the bottom of those commercials with starving African children, saying, "Warning: Taking action may lead to serious mental health risks." But it's true. At least, in my experience and what I've seen in others. And no one wants to talk about that—how justice can consume you (not in a good way), how it keeps you up at night, how it becomes an obsession.

If we are not careful, we may end up living like Martha, the woman who was so content to do things for Jesus that she forgot why she was doing them in the first place. Yes, friends, compassion can become a distraction. The needs are so abundant that it seems selfish to consider our own spiritual health while seeking to do good in the world. But that is exactly what we must do if we are going to be more than do-gooders in the world. If we are going to participate in redemption.

Whenever I think of walking away, I always think of my friend Colleen. Colleen read a book about poverty and immediately felt compelled to help the poor. Like a lot of people, she was overwhelmed with the needs. So she tried to meet them all.

Colleen signed up to volunteer at every shelter, soup kitchen, and social service in Nashville. She was incredibly committed. She was resolved to not do this halfway; it would be her life. She helped people in need with every spare moment she had. Every evening and Saturday afternoon, even Sundays after church, were dedicated to helping the less fortunate. She loved the opportunity to help and learn from others more experienced than her. She was an inspiration of love and perseverance. Or so I thought.

For years, Colleen befriended prostitutes, visited widows, and delivered food to the handicapped. She invited homeless people into her home and her life. She read every book, watched every movie and adopted every discipline. She was beyond focused. However, she began to realize that some of the problems she was battling were big, complicated issues that required holistic solutions. She began to realize that some of these people needed more than a warm bed or a nice conversation over coffee. They needed help at a deep level that she couldn't provide. This was something she didn't know how to give. And it wrecked her.

Colleen did what most of us would do. She tried harder. She

redoubled her efforts and focused on fewer projects. She read and studied harder so she could handle any issue. Yet she still ended up feeling stressed and burned out. On top of that, her marriage was starting to suffer. Instead of bringing healing to the brokenness around her, Colleen was being broken herself.

The kind of brokenness we're talking about here is not healthy. It's not the spiritual brokenness you hear about in church or at Bible studies. It's dysfunctional. It's painful in a way that disrupts the healthy systems in your life. And that's exactly what was happening to my friend Colleen—everything around her was falling apart. All because of her compassion. Something had to change.

Colleen had to step down from all weekly volunteer commitments. This was her choice, but it was still hard. She began concentrating on "smaller" things: serving at church, befriending neighbors, and loving her husband. It was a paradigm shift for her, a discipline. But it was one she needed to make.

Shortly after Colleen scaled back her volunteering, I met with her over coffee. She told me what she was doing with all the extra time and energy she normally would've spent volunteering at soup kitchens. She was now investing in her marriage. She was reading books and asking people's advice on how to love her husband well. She was spending most nights and weekends with him instead of serving on the streets.

By serving the poor, Colleen had learned how much she could give of herself to something she was passionate about. And for the first time, she was applying that to immediate relationships she had neglected. "It's so good," she told me. I believed her. In fact, I was envious. My friend had stumbled upon something I hadn't yet grasped—that we are only able to help heal the brokenness around us when we are living whole lives ourselves. When we neglect the systems and structures that are intended to bring us life, we not only rob ourselves and those around us, but we also rob those to whom we would minister. In other words, you can't forsake everything for the cause of justice; it will undermine the stability you need to heal the poor and hurting.

I know a lot of people who are passionate about social justice, and most of them would admit that not being able to serve is uncomfortable. "I can't just do nothing!" they might say. But sometimes, that is exactly what we are called to do—to be still and know there is a deeper story happening, one that goes beyond what we could do with our own hands and feet.

This is no excuse to not act, but it's a caution to steward our lives well. If we do not, we may be forced to give up something good for a season. So that we can be made whole. So that we can grow up. This is what God wants from us—not to serve out of our brokenness (although we all start there), but to serve as whole people, helping others heal and find wholeness. Anything else is codependence, a sham to assuage our guilt.

Being able to walk away is a sign of maturity. When we first discover the world's needs, we become consumed with righting every wrong we see. We put our passion to work, every spare minute doing whatever we can to help "the cause." But exhausting yourself on behalf of the poor and downtrodden will ultimately burn you out physically, emotionally, and spiritually. When this happens, it becomes hard to pray. We may even resent God for not doing something, as I did with Michelle. We may strive harder to fill the gaps. We may neglect our families, churches, work, and even ourselves. In the process, we may become the brokenness we seek to heal.

Trying to be effective in everything means not being effective in anything. My friend Colleen discovered this when she was bouncing from one volunteer opportunity to the next. She wasn't volunteering as much as she was making an appearance. She was busy, but not effective. Certainly, there are enough needs in the world to keep us busy, but without being intentional, we will do little long-term good.

WHEN TO NOT WALK AWAY

It's hard to let go of those initial thrills, to do the difficult, mature work of being present to those around us. This is not easy, but it's necessary to making an impact on the world. As we get healthy, though, we should not be surprised that God may call us to commit to certain things. This is, after all, what it means to be wrecked—to intentionally step into discomfort and live in that tension.

In other words, sometimes we don't walk away. Not when it really matters. How do we know when to stay and when to walk away? We know it's time to stay when running away is precisely what we want to do.

Detached. That's how I felt when I looked at a man with a busted nose, and he asked me for help. At first, I pretended I didn't hear him. Then I justified why it wasn't wise to help him.

That's not even why we came down here, I thought.

I had done my good deed for the day. My friend Paul and I met James that night no more than thirty minutes after he had his nose broken in a fight. Another guy had head-butted him in the face. In his words, "That just ain't right." There were pools of blood all over the place that served as signposts marking where James had been. Every once in a while, the blood would stop flowing, and he would sneeze up a clot, spurting blood in all directions. It was disgusting.

We were under the street again, spending time with our new friends. James. Cheeseburger. A woman I didn't recognize who was clinging closely to the man with the broken nose. There were a few others nearby.

We helped bring James up to the surface and told him to stay put. Then we went in search of a police officer or ambulance, whichever came first. We ran into Jimbo, another homeless man we had recently met. He was wearing the boots I brought him the previous week. Jimbo was suffering from heart problems. He said he had open-heart surgery a while back, and that his heart was acting up again. He could barely walk, and it was obvious that he was more than just inebriated. He asked us to call 911. We told him to stay with James, and we quickened our steps.

I had no idea where we were going or what we would do once we got there. I was scared and still distancing myself emotionally from the whole situation. There was a coldness to my heart that was being shaken.

We prayed loudly and desperately that God would show us the way. Our spoiled suburban mindsets were telling us not to go "too far" for a couple of bums not entitled to the benefits of the system. We turned a corner and almost ran into an ambulance. It was parked right outside of a fire department, but we couldn't find any way to get in. We knocked and shouted, but no one answered.

I spotted a parked police car up another block. We hurried but found no police officer. Instead, we came upon a security officer who was writing a parking ticket. We told him the situation, and he gave us a number to call. A nonemergency number. Would no one help us?

We headed back, still on hold with the dispatch. By the time we connected, we could see the guys waiting for us where we told them to stay. I was surprised they had listened. They must have really needed the help. During the time we had been gone (probably close to thirty minutes), James had stopped bleeding and started again. He kept cussing and saying how he was going to kill the guy who did this to him.

Jimbo kept rambling about his new boots, which he loved. Even under the circumstances, I had to smile. Minutes later, a fire truck arrived and the paramedics immediately went to work. They loaded up James on a stretcher, while he kept coughing and sneezing up blood. The paramedic told him, "Don't talk; I don't want you to spit blood in my face."

I noticed that several people around James had all backed up. I was one of them. We all shared a look of fear and apprehension in our eyes, as this man from the street spit contagions into the air. We who were clean backed away from the dirty man—all except one. It was the woman who was with him when we found him under the walkway. She used her white sleeve to wipe away the blood from his face. She held his hand as they strapped him in, and she asked if she could go with him.

I realized I was still afraid of these people. Still thought I was better than them. Shame on me.

When I think about what it means to love people, to really, truly love those who don't deserve it, I think of that woman. Her relatively clean sweatshirt stained with James's blood—that image is imprinted into my mind forever. I don't mean to sound trite, but it makes me think of Jesus, who loved people not by "getting down on their level," but by being on the same level. He ministered to the poor by being poor. He loved the homeless by being homeless.

If we want to understand the secret to living a good life—to loving people like this—we have to be willing to do the unthinkable. We have to get dirty. We cannot be afraid of the cost, of getting stained with someone else's filth. We cannot avoid the walls that divide us—the superficialities and prejudices that separate the "clean" from the "unclean." All those need to fall down, to disappear, if we are going to stop playing around and actually do this. Otherwise, we should just stop kidding ourselves.

When you meet someone whose needs you can't meet—whether it's a busted nose or a drug addiction—you experience a different kind of wrecking. You feel incapable of doing the one thing you long to do, which is help. These encounters force you to give up on the hope that you can resolve every conflict you encounter within twenty-four hours. And you realize that in order to truly effect change, you have to sometimes walk away. Not for the sake of abandoning someone, but in order to do something of lasting value.

CHAPTER 8

Get a JOB

"A building has integrity just like a man. And just as seldom."
— AYN RAND

Missionary jaunts and short-term missions are not enough to change the world. They're not enough to leave an impact. Sure, short-term experiences are valuable for the initial "wrecking" that needs to happen—the rending of your heart to help you see the world differently. But eventually you need to commit to a cause. You need to find your role in the world and stick with it. To make a true difference, you need something more permanent. You need to settle. Not in a bad way, but in the best way. You need to get a job. To grow up.

When I was finishing up my yearlong commitment with a mission organization after college, a friend asked me, "What's next for you?" This is, by the way, the question everyone asks at the end of a journey—and nobody ever knows the answer.

I told her, without pausing, "Probably the hard thing." I went on to explain I had multiple opportunities—in Missouri, California,

Georgia, and even China. "But I'll probably end up doing the thing that I don't want to do." This may sound masochistic, but it's not. I was beginning to understand something about life: Sometimes, what's hard is what's right. So I moved to Tennessee to "see about a girl" and slept in a friend's living room for seven months, while working two part-time jobs. It wasn't glamorous. It wasn't easy. It wasn't even superspiritual or sexy. But it was good.

We learn commitment by doing hard things. We die a little to our ambitions so we can live like we were meant to. Nothing does this like a real job that requires you to show up and do work that others are counting on.

WHEN OTHERS ARE COUNTING ON YOU

Matt Snyder and I worked together for two years. For the first six months, every other week he told me he wanted to quit. He had just returned from a year of adventures around the world, so it was understandable that he was restless. But after a while, I'd had enough. I couldn't take any more complaining. I told him to either leave or shut up.

The next day, Matt called me with the news I was expecting to hear. He told me he wanted to leave, but he added an interesting caveat: if I wanted him to stay, he would. I'd not been a boss that long, and this felt odd. But I wanted to be vindicated. I had resolved to fire him, but I gave it a day to consider.

The next day, I did something that surprised even me: I held Matt to his original commitment to work for us for twelve months. I don't know why I did this. It just felt right, like Matt needed to learn something important. Years later, during his exit interview, he told me, "The last thing I wanted from you was for you to hold me to my word, but it was one of the best things anyone's ever done for me."

Matt is the hero of this story, not me, because he did something most people refuse to do: he stuck it out. He did something longer than he wanted to. As a result, he did great, meaningful work that we all benefited from, and he learned a valuable lesson in the process. So did I. After we had that talk, Matt never complained about his job. I think he actually started to like it. And it showed, because the quality of his work became astoundingly better.

When we constantly seek our own happiness, we're rarely satisfied. But when we let go out of immediate gratification and serve others, we find ourselves truly enjoying life. Commitment causes us to grow in a weird way. We find ourselves by losing, by giving up our own rights. The child in us would rather hide and dodge responsibility, but instead we lean in and persevere. And ultimately we benefit, like Matt did.

Our team and organization benefited from thousands of hours of meaningful work Matt did, work that affected hundreds of lives. To think he almost didn't do that is amazing. This is why we step into commitment, why we stick with a job longer than we'd like. Because sometimes that feeling of discomfort isn't intuition; it's fear. And we need to face it, head on, and overcome it. We need to commit, not only because it's what we need, but because it's what the world needs.

YOU NEED MORE THAN AN EVENT

I recently interviewed Scot McKnight, a college professor in Chicago, and asked him what his number one concern for young people was. He said too many young adults are chasing events and experiences when they should be developing habits that lead to a lifestyle. He was speaking directly to me.

With a few exceptions, most of us won't work a different job every day. Jobs don't work like that; they're more long-term. If they did, we would never get good at anything and wouldn't make much of an impact. A job is not an event; it's more of a lifestyle. So why do we often treat compassion like an experience, relegated to Saturday afternoon serve days with our church and weeklong journeys into the developing world?

I am more guilty of this than most.

One Saturday, I met Pat, a woman battling cancer. She had no car, no money, no food. She was living in an apartment near the airport and was about to be evicted. I made a connection with her when we met, so I started visiting her on a regular basis.

About once a week, I would bring Pat food and listen to her story, always told in a thick Bostonian accent, roughed up from years of smoking. She would tell me about the Jehovah's Witnesses she visited—how she didn't believe in everything they believed but loved how they studied the Bible. We'd talk about her dogs and the government and how terrible public aid was.

One month, Pat couldn't pay her rent, so some friends and I chipped in to help her stay off the streets, a place she had, unfortunately, lived before.

"I ain't goin' back there," she told me, resolutely.

I nodded in agreement. *No, you ain't.* I wasn't doing much beyond helping Pat meet a temporary need. She knew this. I knew it. But what else could we do?

Eventually I stopped visiting Pat. I got busy, and she stopped answering her phone. We lost touch. This is not something I'm proud of; I should've visited her more, should've reached out again. But I didn't. I left Pat. I am ashamed of this, but I am most embarrassed by the fact that I didn't try to connect her with others who could have helped her in the long-term. I tried to be the Lone Ranger, the sole savior. I wanted to be her Messiah. And in the end, I failed. So will you, if you think of compassion like I did: as a series of individual experiences. What I needed was a way of thinking about helping people in a more long-term way.

I used to be a skeptic of short-term missions. I didn't think they did any good. After a fifteen-day trip to Mexico, though, I became a believer. In those two short weeks, I saw churches planted, paralyzed people healed, and a community revived. I believe in the potential of short-term missions. That's why it's hard to say this: short-term missions are not enough.

Short-term missions are a means to an end. And the end is connection. We are connecting our hearts to the needs of the world. But if that connection doesn't lead to deeper change—in those serving and being served—it's pointless. Long-term change and transformation is what we're going for here. Not a subculture addicted to short-term commitments that leave a temporary high, only to be replaced by skepticism and an emotional gap to be filled next summer. Short-term missions can wreck us, but if the means becomes the end, then we have failed.

This disillusionment with short-term experiences is why I stopped lurking the streets to find homeless people to love and started volunteering at the mission. It was humbling and hard, but worth it. Since I met Micah on the streets of Spain, I had always wanted to do something special that involved serving the needy. But in Nashville, I learned a crucial lesson: compassion is a full-time vocation; as such, it needs to be treated seriously. You can be a freelancer, always searching for your next project on the horizon, or you can join an organization dedicated to long-term ministry. The latter is far more effective.

When I first visited the mission, I felt like a sell-out. Like I was doing the "easy" thing by volunteering at a mission instead of being the on-the-streets "radical" I wanted to be. It offended my entrepreneurial sense, but frankly, I was tired of getting burned—of connecting with people on the streets only to see them disappear weeks later. I was tired of being lied to and of seeing people I loved go through the same painful patterns over and over again. So I decided to try someone else's method.

Josh Darnell, one of the staff members at the Nashville Rescue Mission, told me he ministered on the streets for years. Why then, I asked, was I talking to him in a brick-and-mortar building, where he worked with homeless men going through a program? Because, he explained, meeting men on their own turf was not enough. While you might be able to have a great conversation on the street, there was no commitment on either side. In order to see full transformation, Josh learned, you have to introduce some kind of control. You have to get broken people out of a bad environment long enough to help them. That's why he started working at the mission. And that's why I joined him.

FROM AWAKENING TO APPLICATION

My friend Matthew Paul Turner recently told me about how he takes bloggers on World Vision trips to some of the poorest areas in the world. When I asked him what happens after the trips, he said people experience a sort of reverse culture shock. They struggle with things as simple as going to the grocery store or visiting the mall. There are so many in need that the excess they return to is overwhelming.

I asked Matthew how the experiences of going overseas multiple times a year, visiting communities in Africa and Latin America, affected him. He said that after a while he started to feel numb, which for him is a good thing. If you're going to make an impact, at some point you need to look past the initial shock of tragedy. You need to move beyond the pain—forget discomfort, dig in, and do the work. Here's what he said:

In order for that first wrecked experience to continue to change me, I must proactively seek to become broken again and again. "Need" exists all around us. While it's of utmost importance to do all we can to help the impoverished people in other places, it's also important for us to let those short-term experiences help shape how we see our here and now. While every trip I take moves me and breaks me on many levels, I doubt that I'll ever encounter the type of breaking I experienced that first time in Romania. And I hope I don't. Because that experience was about me, about my heart changing, about my eyes being opened. That is the experience that makes me want to pursue less stuff and live sustainably. But the wrecking that happens now, when I witness poverty and injustice, my prayer is that God will use those experiences to help me bring change for them, help me to provide the basic things that they need. I have to fight against the temptation to make the experience about me, about all that I have, about "Americanisms" and the like. But fighting against Americanisms doesn't help the little boy I met in Bolivia who needs a hearing aid. I could weep and become emotional (and there's nothing wrong with those things—they are needed at times) all day long for that kid, or I could say, "Can I buy him that hearing aid?" and allow my "wrecking" to help him hear. It's a balancing act in some ways. All of us need that first wrecking, we need it to be about us, to make us question everything, to break us of our selfish ways. But then we need the wreckings we experience to help us change the realities for the people and stories and faces and injustices that are wrecking us.

Being wrecked is about us, but compassion is about others. You can't stay wrecked forever; you eventually have to move on. Choosing to do so may be the greatest wrecking we experience.

My friend Kari, who is a missionary in Uganda, has a different experience with this same truth. After years of serving widows in Africa, she has grown accustomed to what she has seen. The morning we talked, she told me the government had just bulldozed an entire community. They wanted the land, so they took it. I asked if she felt desensitized, if after a while you just grow numb to these sorts of things: poverty, pain, injustice.

"No, not desensitized," she said. "Just not surprised." Being desensitized means the situation doesn't affect you like it used to, she told me, that it doesn't break your heart anymore. "And that's just not true," she said.

When something traumatic happens to you, you go into shock, a temporary state of numbness. It happened to me once, when I cut my hand on a tape measure. At first, I didn't notice the pain. This allowed me to wrap up my hand and arrange a visit to the hospital. Then the pain came—a slow, steady throb. I still have the scar. In my case, the shock helped me handle the situation, but of course, it can be really dangerous, too. Shock can stun you so badly that you don't do anything. Or it can be used to help. But eventually, the shock goes away, and what remains is what we choose to do with the pain that lingers.

Kari sees things that break her heart every day, things that would shock most of us. But they don't stun her anymore, not like they used to. This lack of surprise allows her to move beyond the initial shock and do something meaningful. The feelings subside, but the pain never fades. One of the advantages to this lack of surprise is it enables Kari to help others. It allows her to not simply be stunned and incapacitated. And it allows her to lead. She has over seventy people—widows, mostly—depending on her. And she has to be strong.

The difference between being desensitized and no longer being surprised is the fact that you still feel something. You see a situation and know that it's wrong. And sometimes the lack of surprise allows you to do something. It will help you deal with things that used to completely wreck you, and if you do it well, you will always feel part of the pain.

Kari told me her organization, Dorcas Widows, recently brought on an intern named Renee. Renee is struggling with what she's seeing and experiencing in Uganda. Simple things like cultural customs and life in Africa are all too much to take in. For a girl from California, it can all feel a bit jarring. But the good news is she's not alone. Here's what Kari told her: "You will feel lonely, you will feel sad, you will feel frustrated, you will get angry…. We can stand with you, but we can't keep it from happening." The truth is this is not about what you feel. Everybody feels something. What lasts is what you do—after the shock wears off, after the feelings fade. You need to step into the pain, move through the fear, and do something that matters.

BUILDING A LEGACY THAT LASTS

Lynne Kurdziel started out her career as most twentysomethings do: with a college degree and high aspirations. She wanted to grow her career and her paycheck, working for big companies, making big money. However, it didn't take long for her to realize how unfulfilling such a pursuit could be.

Lynne discovered a need to build something sooner than most do. She went straight from short-term experience to long-term impact—something we all need to do. Here's Lynne's story in her own words:

> It wasn't long after graduating that I was at a large, few-billion-dollar company, being groomed for upper division management. I had achieved exactly what I wanted: impressive boardroom meetings, important-looking suits, the whole deal. The funny

thing about climbing the corporate ladder was that it wasn't as satisfying as I thought it would be. In fact, nothing about the scenario in the "business world" was that satisfying. Seemed like every day I'd go into work at a shark tank, and the pressure quickly started to make my goals of growing my career and paycheck lose their luster.

Lynne began to realize her life was not about her. She started to see how pointless wealth and prestige are when pursued as an end in and of themselves. Although her career was still important to her, there was a lot happening beneath the surface. In her personal life, she experienced an awakening of sorts. She started getting more involved in church and began changing her outlook on life: "It wasn't long before I started realizing I was made for much more than 'chasing the dollar.'"

Lynne started looking for a new job. She found another opportunity in the corporate world. The company pursued her, and she accepted the offer and left her current job. Two weeks later, though, the opportunity fell through.

Lynne was suddenly unemployed for the next six months with no income or prospects. This time of limbo caused her to search her soul. She recalls, "So there I was, with marketing experience and an interest in doing 'something meaningful' (whatever that meant) with no job and no money." At this point, she started asking important questions: "If I could do absolutely anything and didn't have to worry about money, what would I do? What do I have that the world needs?"

Several weeks later, Lynne had an idea: What if she created a company? What if she built something that provided the level of excellence she was accustomed to in the corporate environment to organizations who had messages worth spreading: ministries, churches, and nonprofits? The thought excited her:

I could help these organizations spread their message, gain funding, and grow their exposure and following! I didn't know anything about starting a company, but just like anything scary, I knew I'd have to just take the plunge. So I did. I set out on my own as an entrepreneur with my "good idea" and not much else. Because I no longer had a salary and didn't have any clients yet (let alone a business model), I had to break my lease early and move out of my apartment.

Over the next few months, Lynne sold all of her belongings on Craigslist and used the money for rent and business startup costs. Fast forward a few years, and now she has a team that helps organizations and businesses tell their stories. She and her team have now worked with forty nonprofits, helping them create brands, communicate their missions, and gain an online presence. She's making a living for herself and helping others in the process. It may not be Madison Avenue, but it's a legacy she can be proud of.

Lynne did something few of us are able to do: she bridged the gap between a fleeting passion and the will to do something that lasts.

QUITTING TIME

There are two types of work: the kind you have to do and the kind you are meant to do. Both can exhaust you. Sometimes you don't know which is which—when it's time to quit and when it's time to persevere. Knowing the difference is key to finding your calling and doing work that matters.

If ever I wanted to quit my vocation, it would have been the other week. I was traveling, maxed out on responsibilities and expectations, attending more meetings than I could bear, and managing multiple projects and people at once. I wanted to scream. On top of that, our organization and my team were in a state of transition. I was getting little sleep, pulling long days, and my body was starting to put up a fight. (When I don't sleep, I get sick.)

Yet, I felt strangely alive.

Don't get me wrong—it was brutal, and I was glad to see the weekend arrive. But there's something strangely invigorating about a week like that. A week full of exhausting yourself on things worth your energy and time.

In the film *The Mexican*, starring Brad Pitt and Julia Roberts, a question is posed and repeated by various characters: "If two people love each other, but they just can't seem to get it together, when do you get to that point of enough is enough?"[25] The implicit answer from the story is this: never. True love never gives up. Never. That's how I feel about all major commitments: my marriage, my family, my friends, and my vocation. What do you do when it's exhausting to pursue your calling? You do it anyway. There's abundance in sticking out a commitment and persevering through the challenges. There's also joy and fulfillment.

In 2010, Haiti was devastated by an earthquake that resulted in one of the greatest natural disasters in the western hemisphere in our lifetime. Our organization responded immediately with humanitarian aid and supplies. People were dying, and the needs were dire. So we had to move quickly. Most of our staff started pulling twelve-hour days. For weeks, I stayed up late and got up early, glued to my computer for nearly every waking moment. Each day hundreds of emails poured in with updates on the catastrophe and what was being done to help. It was hard and exhausting and absolutely worth it. My wife wasn't crazy about the time I was spending working, but she understood the importance of what I was doing. She knew I had a job to do, a commitment to fulfill, and that people were counting on me. So she encouraged me to do it.

During that crazy season, people asked me why I pushed myself so hard, why we all did. I was responsible for sending out press releases and updating a blog that notified our constituents of ways they could bring relief to those affected by the quake. When I wasn't sending out updates, I was on my cell phone talking around the clock with colleagues to figure out what else we could do to help. Yes, it was a lot of work, but it needed to be done. As I poured out myself into this work and exhausted my mental resources, the experience gave me life.

Everyone needs something like what I experienced with the Haiti crisis—not an obsession or excuse to be a workaholic, but a true vocation, a calling. It may not be your day job or even a job at all, but it's there, hiding in your spirit, waiting to be discovered.

Career and calling are not always synonymous. Some things we do—like parenting or making art or falling in love—we do even when we're dead tired and worn out. We push through the exhaustion and do it anyway. Because the thing itself is worth doing. Because that's what a calling is all about. It's not something you choose, but something to which you are called.

The challenge in pursuing a true vocation is not to wait for the thing itself—that will lead to procrastination—but to train yourself in the art of making commitments. Because we don't know when we're going to fall in love, all we can do is prepare for the moment. The same is true for your calling.

You can think of your seasonal commitment or day job as a burden, something to be overcome or resented, or you can think of it as practice for what's to come: your true vocation. Doing the latter will prepare you to love what you do, so that ultimately you can do what you love and actually appreciate it.

That's what getting a job will do for you. It's what it's done for me: taught me how to commit. It's not the perfect job (there's no such thing), but it's the right one for right now. How do I know? Because I'm growing. I'm being pushed and stretched. And as a result, I'm getting wrecked in a whole new way.

CHAPTER 9

GOING Where You
Don't Want to GO

"When you were younger you . . . went where you wanted; but
when you are old . . . someone else will . . . lead you where you
do not want to go."

— JESUS

During the year I traveled the country playing music, older
adults frequently told me, "This is great to do . . . while
you're still young."

While you're still young.

Those words stung. They haunted and frustrated me. They
reeked of dashed dreams and vicarious living, foreboding my
impending, awful adulthood. To be honest, I thought these people
were making excuses. It's easier to not feel guilty for living more
"radically" (because that's what I thought I was doing) if you can
make broad statements that lump certain activities into the "while
you're still young" category.

But now I see those words as the well-intended remarks they
were. Many who uttered them were imparting wisdom. They

were telling me about a reality of life.

When we are young, the world is our oyster. We travel, go on adventures, discover a world we never knew. But life doesn't continue like this forever—not for most of us. We grow up, buy houses, get bosses, and pay bills. Ultimately, we go where we don't want to go. We go where we must, to the places we're called. Although the adolescent within rebels, the adult knows it's right.

When you get older, life sometimes just sort of happens to you. Without your permission or realization, you may end up in a position where you don't have the freedom you once had. You may find yourself locked into commitments you can't get out of. When you get older, people depend on you; you have real responsibility.

So while you're young, do what you want. Because you won't always be able to. You won't always be able to be so carefree.

ENTERING A NEW SEASON

Life is made up of seasons. At certain times, we are supposed to travel and explore our restlessness. At others, we're not. When you're in your twenties, you're sort of between seasons. And it's important to recognize this, if you're going to make the most of the opportunities you have.

Shauna Niequist writes about this in her book *Bittersweet*. "There is a season for wildness and a season for settledness, and this is neither," she writes. "This season is about becoming. Don't lose yourself at happy hour, but don't lose yourself on the corporate ladder either."[26]

My boss, Seth, calls this period of life "a series of internships." You try on different hats, experiment, fail—and you learn. That's what this season is about: becoming who you are.

Eventually, there comes a time to commit, to be who you are

meant to be. Which means making hard choices, even sometimes doing things you don't want to do. This is important, necessary even. For the longest time, I thought this was the great big sell-out moment, the decision that would mortgage my freedom and tether me to empty commitments for the rest of my life. I thought I would end up like a character from *The Office*, rolling my eyes at a humdrum existence. But that's not the case at all.

Sometimes, we need to wait, to listen, to learn. In your journey to find your life's work, you'll have to do the same. For me, this happened when I was twenty-five.

I remember where I was and what I was doing. I was driving to downtown Nashville, where I was still doing some volunteer work at the homeless rescue mission. I had started a full-time job just a few months before and was having trouble balancing my time between that and doing street ministry. My mind was swirling with the possibilities of the future. Although I had a new wife, new job, and a new church, I was tempted to want more. And I was deceived.

Deep within me, there was a whisper—a small, quiet voice, calling me to slow, to take notice of where I was and be present.

I remember it distinctly. It was almost audible. The sense was unmistakable. All my dreams, all my aspirations for myself—these were not going to happen. What I wanted wasn't as important as it used to be. People were counting on me, and I knew God expected more from me than dreaming. He wanted my action.

Again, this was one of those spooky moments where you might think I'm crazy. I certainly did. But I can't deny it. I heard the voice clearly: *This is a season of commitment.* It nearly stopped me dead in my tracks. I'm surprised I didn't hit the brake pedal as I was driving. The words rolled around in my head all day and for the following weeks: *This is a season of commitment.* Over five years later, I'm at the same job, live in the same town, and have the same wife. I've never had that before. What once scared me—the idea of committing to anything for more than a blink of time—is now a comfort and source of confidence. I don't feel trapped; I feel free and enabled to live out the life I'm meant to live. And the best part is I don't have to do it alone.

While you're young, you will make choices that will change the way you see the world. You should stay up late and act impulsively, do a few things you've never done before. Not because the rest of your life is a bore, but because this is what this season is for. In the next, you will have to make other decisions—difficult ones—that will equally define you. You will buy a house or change diapers. You will stick with a job not for a month, but a year, longer than you'd like. All because God is shaping you. He is teaching you to wait, to persevere, to become. This is just as uncomfortable as traveling the world or moving to a new state. Maybe more.

FORMING NEW HABITS

When I was in college, I tried to work out and stay fit. But I wasn't great at it. College life is spontaneous and stressful, full of late-night study sessions, early morning exams, and unexpected emergencies. You have all the time in the world, and if you're bad at managing your time (as I was), this is a terrible freedom. However, I finally got serious about going to the gym during my senior year. A friend and I committed to meeting every other morning to work out and catch up.

One morning in the locker room, I ran into a German professor I knew. I had never taken any classes with him, but we knew each other from foreign language events (I was a Spanish major). The conversation we had has never left my memory—for one, because I wasn't accustomed to conversing in the locker room with another man while we were both changing clothes (that's just against "guy code"), and two, because of the wisdom he shared:

"Good morning," the professor said to me. I grunted in reply. It was somewhere around 6 a.m., and I was still questioning the sanity of this new vow of health my friend and I had made. "What brings you here?" the professor continued.

"Oh. Uh, I'm working out with a friend," I said with my eyes probably closed.

"That's great," he said, "just great. Do you do this often?"

"Uh, yeah. We've been coming for a few weeks now—every other day," I grumbled in an indistinguishable tongue. I was probably speaking German.

"That's great," he repeated, "just great."

He paused, maybe hesitating to say what he said next. I'm glad he did: "You know, the habits you form here will be with you for the rest of your life."

That's when it hit me.

My eyes opened wide, as if a splash of cold water had hit my face. For the rest of the day, those words resonated in my soul. I looked around at what I saw other people doing—what I myself was doing—and wondered: Is this what I want to be doing in ten years?

Years later, I still think about that. It's true, you know. I think about my friends who drank a lot—I mean a *lot*—and how they're still doing that today. Only now it's not called "partying." It has a less glamorous name: alcoholism. I think about the friends who slept around, many of whom ended up getting pregnant and married before graduation. Some are now facing divorce due to infidelity. Yes, there is grace and second chances, but this is a fact of life: the more you do something, the easier it gets. The habits we form, especially at an age when we are completely free to make our own choices, often stick with us for the rest of our lives.

"I DO WHAT I WANT!"

In college, my friends and I had a saying: "I do what I want." It was a male ego thing, I'm certain of it. Anytime someone disagreed with us (usually a girl), we would respond quickly and definitively, "I do what I want!" It was a proclamation of independence, asserting that we were the masters of our own destiny and no one was going to tell us what to do. The problem, though, was it was not true.

We didn't do what we wanted. Because we didn't always want to study or pay tuition, but we did. Why? We had to. This is the reality of being young: you get to do what you want because there isn't a lot you have to do. But rest assured, you do not always do what you want. You do what you have to do. As life goes on, the list of "have to's" gets longer. This can cause you to get bitter, if you're not careful, if you're not prepared for it. But hopefully, you know better.

The apostle Peter was a headstrong guy. Maybe even a little impulsive. He was the fisherman who dropped his nets to follow a rabbi around the country. He was the one who (without thinking, I'm sure) stepped out of a boat and tried walking on water. And he was the one who pulled out a sword and cut off the ear of a Roman soldier. It's safe to say Peter did what he wanted.

Peter was no stranger to responsibility. He was a married man and presumably had held down a steady job. Until he met Jesus. Then he spent three years going on radical adventures and learning about a new way to see the world. Maybe it was a slight case of midlife crisis or just how Peter made decisions, but he didn't seem to think much before deciding. He just acted. All that changed when he was given a job to do for the rest of his life—when Jesus told Peter He was going to build His church on him, the foundation, the rock.

What did this mean for Peter? His rabbi told him, "When you were younger you dressed yourself and went where you wanted; but when you are old you will stretch out your hands, and someone else will dress you and lead you where you do not want to go."[27] As the story goes, Peter was eventually captured and crucified. Some accounts say he insisted on being hanged upside down because he felt unworthy to die in the same manner as Christ. But this means more than how Peter died. It has to do with how he lived the rest of his life.

Peter learned the hard way when he was out of line. More than once, Jesus called him out for his impulsive behavior. He often spoke and acted without thinking. Passion was his driving emotion. Which did a lot of good for him. But it also got him into trouble. Passion led him to follow Jesus in the first place, but it also caused him to rebuke his master and get called "Satan."

As he grew older and matured, Peter learned that a true disciple doesn't always do what he wants to do, doesn't always act on the first impulse. He learned that the greatest sign of a true follower is obedience, not unrestrained zeal. It's maturity. And he exemplified this with his life—eschewing old Jewish customs, like what foods were considered clean or what was acceptable company. He wasn't perfect, but he was a lot more humble. He realized his life no longer belonged to himself.

WHAT DOES THIS MEAN FOR US?

Life, I'm learning, is full of moments of discomfort. And in these moments, we have a choice: we can step into the opportunity they provide for us to grow, or we can shrink back and avoid the pain. I'm trying to do the former, without too many complaints.

We all have to do things that might not come easy to us; the trick is to see the purpose behind them. As a husband, this means making personal sacrifices for my wife because I love her and she deserves it. It means being available to my family—as both a leader and servant. And as an employee, it means trusting my boss and doing the work that is required of me, even when I don't feel like it.

Most importantly, this also means that what God wants in my life is more important than what I want. Now, that has the potential to sound kind of cultish, but the truth is that I can't be trusted with my life. I need some spiritual guidance, or I'm just going to screw things up. Like a child, I'll always end up doing the things I want, but never pursuing the things I need. In my life, every time I've pursued what I wanted, I've ultimately been hurt, disappointed, or heartbroken. Only when I've submitted to a plan bigger than my own—when I've given myself to a cause beyond myself—have I found some piece of true fulfillment.

When I was about to graduate college, I was sure I was going to move to Latin America. As a Spanish major, I figured the next logical step was to speak Spanish for the rest of my life. I had already been to Spain, so it only made sense. My best friend had moved to Guatemala, and I planned to join him. Little did I know I was going to be called where I didn't want to go. I would have to give up my own desires in submission to a larger plan.

I was visiting a church where someone was speaking about the importance of global missions. The presenter talked about things like the 10/40 Window and Haystack Prayer Meeting, and I started to feel guilty for wanting to move to Latin America. At the end of the daylong seminar, I walked up to the speaker and asked to talk. I told him I spoke Spanish and asked if he still recommended people to go to North Africa, the Middle East, and Asia. He told me something that sticks with me even today: "The gifts do not precede the call."

When we look at what we have to offer—our skills, gifts, and desires—before asking what is needed of us, we are putting the cart before the horse, or the gifts before the call. The question a disciple must first ask is not, "What am I good at?" but rather, "What is required of me?"

In my case, this meant surrendering to the possibility of going somewhere people didn't speak Spanish. For a brief stint, I ended up in Taiwan. Finally, I ended up helping other people discover their passions and callings at a short-term missions organization. Every step of the way, there were unique moments when I was asked to obey, not act impulsively. And now I get to respond to what is required of me on a daily basis—not just what I want to do. Want to know the crazy part? I'm okay with it. It's exciting to be caught up into a story bigger than my own.

THE END OF AN ADVENTURE

As I write this, I'm preparing to be a father. My wife and I just announced the news to our friends. By the time you read this, I will be a dad to a baby boy. Something happens when you learn you're going to have a child. It's the same thing that happens when you get married and land your first real job. It's the burden of responsibility, the pressure of expectation, the beauty of someone relying on you.

My wife and I are still processing the transition. When we go to the doctor for a checkup or ultrasound, it becomes real. We start thinking of ourselves as parents and planning for how our lives will change. But after a day or two, those feelings fade. Life begins to feel normal again—until the next visit. It's a wonderful mix of anxiety and excitement, anticipation and disorientation. A new life is counting on us, needing us to provide for it, and we can no longer merely do what we want. We must do what is required of us. And we're better for it.

When you look around at people who have settled down, there are two ways to view the choices they've made. You could say they "sold out" and gave up on their dreams of living an adventure. Certainly that's probably true for some. But you could also choose to see something different: humility. You could see people who surrendered what they wanted to do and started seeing their lives as an offering for others. For some it means they finally stopped chasing a lifestyle that made them look like the hero and just started acting like one. They sacrificed what they wanted for what was right, and they did so gladly.

This is what anyone who has been wrecked can hope for: to be led where you once didn't want to go and actually be glad you get there.

CHAPTER 10

Wrecking
OTHERS

"Always do everything you ask of those you command."
— GEORGE S. PATTON

The hardest part of getting wrecked is what comes after. What happens when the trip is over, the memories fade, and life begins to feel normal again. Things will slow down, priorities will shift, and you'll question yourself, wondering if you've become a sellout. You'll get married, buy a house, have a few kids. Or you'll work a nine-to-five, stop volunteering, and worry you've lost your edge. You'll look back at your early years with nostalgia, read through old journals and scrapbooks with regret. And you'll wonder what happened.

Take heart. This is your biggest adventure yet, if you seize it. You have a chance—the most important opportunity of your life, in fact—to bring people along on the journey. You get to wreck others.

WHEN LIFE GETS "BORING"

After being wrecked, a lot of people struggle with boredom. Their season of adventure ends, and they live in the past or, worse, vicariously through movies and others' stories. But there's an alternative: you can help other people find their purpose, just like you found yours. You can help friends, family members, and total strangers get wrecked. In helping others find their way, you may find more of yours—at least, the next part of the journey.

In most things, those who do the most work get the least amount of credit. This is true in church, at most places of employment, and when it comes to the business of changing the world. It's not fair, but that's how it works.

My friend Erin exemplifies this inequity. I've never met Erin, but she's a friend, nonetheless. We connected online a few years ago when she read a blog post of mine. I was writing about Pat, the woman with cancer who was having trouble with her rent. Although we had never met in real life, Erin was so moved by Pat's story that she sent me a check for $100. It was a simple gesture that spoke volumes about how she approached life and generosity.

The reason Erin was so willing to give was due to a trip she had recently taken to Swaziland, a country with one of the highest HIV/AIDS infection rates in the world. Her entire perspective was changed on that trip. She saw basic human needs for food and shelter not being met, and it caused her to see everything differently. Now, when presented with a need to help (no matter how small), Erin doesn't hesitate to act. Her heart has been beautifully broken. I asked her how so much could change from one short trip, and this was her reply:

> Since I returned from Africa and began telling stories of amazing people I met in Swaziland, I've learned some really crucial

lessons. We connect to the stories of others. We hear about the massive issues of poverty and disease in Africa but feel paralyzed. We hear about a particular orphanage . . . which needs a new roof and we are mobilized to give. If people know of a specific need, they will give. People always humble me with their generosity.

Each one of us has the power to radically change, and sometimes to save, others' lives. You may think I am being dramatic here, but this is plain truth. The Lord created us for community. And community doesn't always take the form we think it does. Faith without works is dead.

When Erin's trip was over, she recognized that her opportunity to change lives wasn't. If anything, her role had just shifted. She went from participant to storyteller and mobilizer. And the same might happen to you. It certainly did to me.

BECOMING A GUIDE

When I felt the call to be a missionary, I thought I would end up traveling the world for the rest of my life. You know, pack my coffin, move to Africa, and have the natives bury me—that sort of thing. But that's not what happened. In fact, that may never happen. After a lot of struggle, I'm okay with that. I'm finally embracing this is not my life; it doesn't belong to me. I'm not the master of my own destiny. I've started to find what I was made to do, and it has little to do with going or staying and a lot more to do with obedience. It took me a long time to understand this. For a season, I kept seeking my own adventures: short-term missions, weekend road trips, even walking the streets of Nashville to find some needy person to help. All of it was about numbing the call to do what I was supposed to be doing in this season and trying to recreate memories long gone.

I sensed my circumstances changing. I was getting married

and accumulating bills. I feared I would be forced to do what I most dreaded: buy a house. Life began to change, and it felt like I was starting something I never signed up for. So I would leave—in the middle of the day or on the weekend. Just take off. I'd go to a park and feed homeless people. I'd take a quick road trip or drive around in the country. I'd do anything to soothe my restlessness, anything to feel alive again.

In retrospect, I think I understand what I was doing. I was trying to recover that youthful part of myself I had lost to adulthood. I wanted to relive my innocence, to feel like I felt during that first trip to Spain, that first time I turned around and allowed a broken world to break my heart. But the call was changing, evolving. I was no longer supposed to face the brokenness "out there." I was having to deal with the nastiness of my own selfish heart.

> WHAT IT REALLY MEANS TO BE WRECKED IS THAT YOU DO THE HARD THING.

The radical act I was being called to commit to was the one thing I dreaded more than anything: to be normal. So I tried to rekindle my adventurous spirit through minijaunts and reckless wandering. Here's what happens anytime you try to do that: it doesn't work. I like what C. S. Lewis says about it:

It is simply no good trying to keep any thrill: that is the very worst thing you can do. Let the thrill go—let it die away—go on through that period of death into the quieter interest and happiness that follow—and you will find you are living in a world of new thrills all the time. But if you decide to make thrills your regular diet and try to prolong them artificially, they will all get weaker and weaker, and fewer and fewer, and you will be a bored, disillusioned old man for the rest of your life. . . . It is much better fun to learn to swim than to go on endlessly (and hopelessly) trying to get back the feeling you had when you first went paddling as a small boy.[28]

Go back to the house you grew up in, and you'll find that everything feels smaller. The paint is fainter than you recall, the backyard less adventurous. Everything seems so ordinary. Was this really once a castle, a spaceship, the great wild frontier? An historic battlefield? The lost world, full of dinosaurs and danger? Not quite. It probably feels duller. Less mystical. The same thing happens when you watch an old favorite movie—it's not as good as you remember.

Something deep is at work here, something profoundly spiritual.

In the film *Henry Poole Is Here*, the main character (played by Luke Wilson) is so plagued by inner demons that he returns to his childhood neighborhood. At first you don't know why Henry's willing to pay twice the market rate for the house he's buying or why he keeps passing the same house over and over again. Eventually, you discover he's dying, and this is where he wants to be. Why? "It's the last place I remember being happy," he says.[29]

When Henry arrives, the feelings of emptiness and depression don't go away. In fact, they only get worse. This is the lesson we all learn when trying to go back to a feeling in the past that's no longer there. Whether it's holding on to a relationship for too long; returning to a favorite vacation spot; or dreaming of going back to the first job we actually enjoyed, regardless of the pay; trying to prolong a "high" from adolescence or recreate an old memory—it won't work. Like Henry, you'll be disappointed. You'll find that fulfillment doesn't come from what you do or where you live.

This is how you felt the last time you did something for the first time. It wasn't the circumstance that felt so thrilling; it was something inside of you coming alive. So what do you do when this happens? How do you overcome the blues that accompanies every post-wrecked experience? How do you fight the feeling of letdown and disappointment of growing up?

You do what Henry did. You bring someone else along for the journey.

RETURNING HOME

What it means to be wrecked—what it really means—is that you do the hard thing. You step into discomfort. When you bought that plane ticket or moved overseas or took that first trip to the inner city, you were fearful, anxious of the unknown. What wrecked you was the decision to move through that uneasiness and embrace what you didn't know. It was an act of courage—doing the right thing, regardless of how you felt. And this is how life is. It's the same lesson learned over and over again: *Life is not about you.*

Years ago, my friend David was telling me what it was like to be a dad. "Which was harder," I asked, "having your second child, or your third?"

He sighed. "A lot of people ask me that, but the truth is that the biggest adjustment is having your first kid. You know, all of this—marriage, buying a house, having kids—these are all lessons in dying to yourself."

That's it—dying to self. Giving up your rights. Letting go of expectation. This is the lesson we must learn over and over again: true abundance is about giving away your life, about letting go and giving up. It has nothing to do with where you are or what you do; those are catalysts, glimpses at a larger world you've yet to embrace. And as you embrace it, you will be tempted to camp out, to get comfortable. Which is exactly what you must resist doing.

When you're twenty-two, getting wrecked may mean

abandoning your job and traveling the world. It may mean leaving the suburbs and moving to the city or breaking up with your boyfriend and moving cross-country. It may be spurning the corporate climb and taking a position with a local nonprofit. When you're thirty-five, doing the uncomfortable thing may mean cleaning the house or paying the bills. It may look like making sure the kids aren't late for school or that you don't miss a soccer game. It's less glamorous, but the lesson is the same: your life is not about you.

Being wrecked does not look the same for the rest of your life. It changes with the seasons because each season in life has its own set of challenges and temptations. Your goal is to face them with courage and humility, always looking for the thing you're resisting and moving through it. Because that's where the growth happens.

Our life is not supposed to be about what we think will make for an interesting story. It's about pouring out the gifts we've been given for the benefit of others. This may mean living in a leper colony in India or raising five kids in Oklahoma. It may mean relocating to the inner city and starting a homeless outreach center or taking dinner to your neighbor. The important part is to embrace the call, whatever it is, and not merely resign to it. The latter will create resentment and lead to midlife crises, while the former will set you free.

We've all heard that it doesn't matter what you do as much as how you do it. That God can use you anywhere. That you never know what seeds you are planting in people's lives, even when you can't see the fruit. All this is true, but only if you're not using these statements to justify your life. To avoid doing the hard thing—the really radical act that will force you to give up your own rights and submit to a story bigger than your own. If starting a family in the town you grew up in accomplishes this, great. But if it's just a way to hide from what you're really called to do, try again. The point is discomfort. If you're completely complacent, then you're probably missing out.

ON FEELING LIKE A FAKE

As your life begins to stabilize and the things you do begin to feel normal, you may begin to battle inner voices of doubt that will assail you. These types of attacks hit stay-at-home parents and cubicle dwellers the most. Sometimes we use comfort to hide; other times, it's actually adventure that is the escape.

Eventually you may find yourself knee-deep in your life's purpose, living out the story you've been called to live and wondering if you're secretly a fake. You are leading others but have, in fact, lost yourself. That's how I felt when I began telling other people's stories. Who was I? What authority did I have? With my own inner demons and brokenness, what qualified me? I was preaching a message I struggled to follow. At times like these, you may be tempted to give up, but that's exactly what you can't do.

We all hit roadblocks. We fight valiantly and live honorably for years, and then unexpectedly, we get stuck. It may be something seemingly innocuous like an addiction to technology, or it may be something more overt, like drinking too much or looking at pornography. Whatever it is, the obsession inserts itself into our everyday lives, quietly lulling us to sleep. Without noticing, we stop paying attention to our inner life. The world around us begins to feel rote and meaningless. We have to motivate ourselves to do work we used to love. So we distance ourselves from the very structures that could save us—from our families, communities, and those who care most about us. Then we feel guilty for our callousness, which only further alienates us.

This is when you need to be reminded that this is not your

call. This vocation of helping others find their way is not a bright idea you once had. It's something much more. Of course, you may have been operating from your own reservoir for years, but that makes no difference. The original call—the true one—still beckons you to obey. It says this is not your fight. Not yours alone. And it's time to give it back. Yes, get healthy, but also get on with the work. It's not time to give up; it's time to press on.

This epiphany may occur at the height of arrogance or at the depths of brokenness. Wherever and whenever it occurs, it *will* come. And when it does, submit to it. Don't resist or dismiss it. Give in. This voice speaking up inside your heart is not coincidence. It's still, but nonetheless important. Listen to it. It's telling you that you are not alone.

You may find yourself, as I did, allowing these words to pierce your heart: "By the strength of my hand I have done this, and by my wisdom, because I have understanding."[30] *Yes, that's me, believing I've done this all on my own.* We all lose heart at times, wondering if we're qualified to live out the hand we've been dealt. But this is actually a wonderful place to be, because it means going back to the root cause, the reason you began this journey in the first place. Maybe, like me, you will take great comfort in these words: "Does the ax raise itself above the person who swings it, or the saw boast against the one who uses it? As if a rod were to wield the person who lifts it up, or a club brandish the one who is not wood!"[31]

No, it does not.

You are the tool. The mouthpiece. The vessel. You do not get to say when the message is complete. You must only proclaim what you know to be true. Yes, you need to be concerned about integrity—not because of your own reputation, but because of what's at stake here. You need to allow grace to move, especially when you feel at your wit's end, as if you're a total fake. But this work is bigger than you, and this is just another form of the wrecking that happens in your life. Embrace it and overcome it. There's more work yet to do.

ENTERING THE MESS OF LIFE

I visited the Rescue Mission in downtown Nashville one Tuesday morning. I greeted my friends whom I hadn't seen in three weeks due to vacation, work trips, and the busyness of life. I loved being there, away from the pretense of suburban life. It just felt more real. After the stifling facade of "put-together" people, it was refreshing. Every once in a while, you just need raw, unadulterated authenticity. And what better place to find it than in a crowd of drunks, schizophrenics, and perverts? What better place to find God?

That morning at around 10 a.m., the sun and stars must have lined up perfectly, because every competent person mysteriously disappeared from the office, leaving me in a squeaky pleather chair to manage the front desk. As the fates conspired against my destiny, in walked an African-American man who had a disturbed look on his face.

"Uh . . . yeah, 'scuse me?" he said. I looked at him for a moment. He was sweating profusely. *Of course he is,* I thought; *it's ninety-seven degrees out there.* It was June, and June is hot in Tennessee. *Very* hot.

"What can I do for you, sir?" I said, trying to sound professional.

"Yeah. Well, uh, I was wondering, uh, if I could get some pants." He looked a little awkward. I noticed he was sweating a lot—even now, inside the building. I also saw he had one hand behind himself, holding up the rear of his pants.

"Sorry, man," I said, dropping the professionalism. I shook my head in an authoritarian manner. "We don't give out clothes until three. You'll have to wait until then." The disturbed look on his face worsened, and he started to sweat even more.

"Uh, well, you see, it's sort of an emergency. I, uh . . ." he trailed off, continuing to sweat. The guy was starting to make me nervous. I stared at him questioningly, waiting for him to finish. "Well, uh, I kind of, uh, used the bathroom on myself." It took a second for me to process.

I thought: *Big deal. So your pants are wet. Deal with it.*

I told him I had to wait for someone to return before I could see if I could help him. He nodded, turned around and stepped away from the doorway, but still he hung around outside the office. As he turned around, I saw a big brownish stain on the back of his pants, right below where his hand was holding his belt loop. He waited a few minutes. No one came. A few more minutes passed, and I started to sweat. As people would walk by, they would start violently coughing and gagging.

I stepped outside the office and into the hall to meet an awful stench. I remember that smell. It was the smell of the morning after a late-night frat party. It was the smell of our college dorm toilets on a Saturday morning. My friends and I referred to the odor as the smell of "beer farts." But this man hadn't just broken wind. The smell was overwhelming, and I, ashamedly, asked him to step outside and wait for me, enduring the heat of summer.

Seven or eight minutes later, someone finally returned to the office to relieve me. I went to talk to one of the supervisors, explained the situation, and saw the internal battle between mercy and justice in his head play out on his face. It was "just" to make the guy wait until three so that he learned not to defecate in his own pants, but it was merciful to give him (and those around him) some relief.

Finally, I received clearance to get the man some pants. I met him in the bathroom and handed the trousers to him. He smiled, giving me a grateful "thanks" as he hurriedly started to change. I nodded as my eyes watered and the fumes of diarrhea attacked my nostrils. I left as quickly as I could. I walked away and thought without any intention of being tongue-in-cheek: *What a mess.*

I thanked God for it.

I thanked Him that I didn't shy away, even though it was well beyond my personal comfort level. I was grateful for the opportunity to show grace when everything inside of me wanted to do the opposite. I thanked the good Lord for showing me that mercy in the face of trial is always better than shame.

I realized this story is a tad gross, so forgive the dirty details. But let's be honest. These messy, inglorious situations are the ones we don't talk about enough. In church, at work, over a cup of coffee—we avoid these types of tales. But here's the interesting part: They're the ones that matter most. They're real. And they remind us all of our own discomfort, which we avoid and try to hide.

Life is messy. I'm tired of pretending otherwise. We are all that man. At some point, we all face a point in our lives when our shame is laid bare for all to see. If we're lucky, someone comes to our aid, shows us grace.

Hours after giving the man his pants, I saw him again in the lunch line. I had already forgotten his face. He looked me dead in the eyes—as serious as could be—and said, "Hey, thank you." And that was it. Although I hope this man never forgets being bailed out of embarrassment, I know that I'll never forget it. Next time a messy situation comes my way, I'll remember that pair of pants. And I hope I won't shy away. I hope the situation doesn't have to come to me—that I will have enough courage to actually find a mess and step in it.

This is what we're all called to do: find the next mess. This is what it means to be wrecked.

LIVING IN THE PAST

Sometimes I get stuck living in the past. I imagine myself giving homeless men blankets on the streets of Nashville. I recall how my church helped give Michelle's family a beautiful Christmas. Or I dream of simpler days of walking through Seville. But this is all a distraction. It's stalling that keeps me from living in reality now.

What you did years ago doesn't matter. What matters is what you do today, how you're making a difference now. The voice in your head that says you've done enough or that you can be content with one isolated good deed is a lie. It's your enemy, preventing you from being open to how you can be used today. It's a subtle form of sabotage, of deceiving you into believing that life is about you. It's not.

There is a flip side to this issue. Sometimes those inner promptings of feeling like you could do more are actually right on target. They're spiritual indicators telling you that you've veered off course. You've become what you once wished you'd never be. The tendency and temptation is to ignore the voice, to dismiss it as nostalgia. Don't. Your memories of a trip long passed or a life of service and sacrifice may be the very thing you need to get unstuck and move forward.

All of this is about making your life matter, not growing satisfied with your accomplishments. It's about embracing the journey of being brokenhearted for a broken world and allowing it to shape you. It's about navigating through life with open hands, willing to be interrupted. This never goes away. You must always be available. Whenever you sense the call to slow down, to settle, you need to run. Fast and far.

Don't get me wrong: this isn't a matter of beating yourself up or trying to be good enough. That's how we got into this mess in the first place. Rather, it's about living in the tension of a broken world and being content with the journey, not conjuring some contrived sense of arriving.

So what do you do? How do you move through this tension, avoiding shame and inaction alike? It's simple but hard. The answer is this: act. In some small way. Because your memories are not enough. All you have is today. It was all you were ever promised. Yesterday is in the past, and it may be glorious or grisly. But it's gone. And it's time to move on. There is a reason you have air in your lungs today, why you can move your hands or feet—or if you're lucky, both. You were meant to change the world—in some small or big way. What you're called to do is not yours to decide. What is your call is how you respond. Everything you do matters. So do something. Anything. Just move. With God's help and an open heart, you will find the way.

You are leaving a legacy. Whatever you are doing, you are building something that will last. It may be a legacy of action or inaction. It's happening right now. You may not be able to see it, but it's there. You can embrace this or ignore it. But you are still leaving something behind. For your friends. Maybe your children. And perfect strangers who may never know what you did (or didn't do).

My advice? Go for broke. Choose the hard option. Do what comfort screams "no" to—what will ultimately shape you and help others. It may be counterintuitive or against what you've been taught, but do it anyway. Step into inconvenience. Welcome the anxiety that comes with doing the right choice. And be wrecked once again.

NOTES

1. Jim Uhls and Chuck Palahniuk, *Fight Club*, directed by David Fincher (Los Angeles, CA: Fox 2000 Pictures, 1999).

2. John Bunyan, *The Pilgrim's Progress from this World to that Which Is to Come, Delivered under the Similitude of a Dream* (Public Domain Books, 2006).

3. Emily Dickinson, "Success Is Counted Sweetest," accessed March 8, 2012, http://www.poemhunter.com/poem/success-is-counted-sweetest/.

4. Boudleaux Bryant, "Love Hurts," performed by Nazareth, *Hair of the Dog* (c) 1975 Mooncrest and A&M.

5. Incubus, "Love Hurts," *Light Grenades* (c) 2006 Epic.

6. Po Bronson, *What Should I Do with My Life?* (New York: Random House, 2002), accessed March 8, 2012, http://www.pobronson.com/WSIDWML_Introduction.htm.

7. Philippians 3:19.

8. Tony Gilroy, *The Bourne Identity*, directed by Doug Liman (Universal City, CA: Universal Pictures, 2002).

9. Robert Epstein, *Teen 2.0: Saving Our Children and Families from the Torment of Adolescence* (Fresno, CA: Linden Publishing, 2010).

10. J. R. R. Tolkien, *Lord of the Rings* (Boston: Mariner Books, 2005), accessed March 8, 2012, http://www.goodreads.com/quotes/show/137661.

11. G. K. Chesterton, *Orthodoxy* (Public Domain Books, 1994).

12. Brennan Manning, *Ruthless Trust: The Ragamuffin's Path to God* (SanFrancisco: HarperCollins, 2002).

13. Randall Wallace, *Braveheart*, directed by Mel Gibson (Icon Entertainment, 1995).

14. John 12:24.

15. This quotes is often misattributed as: "Most men lead lives of quiet desperation and go to the grave with the song still in them." The actual quote is from Henry David Thoreau, *Walden*. http://www.walden.org/Library/Quotations/The_Henry_D._Thoreau_Mis-Quotation_Page.

16. Andy and Larry Wachowski, *The Matrix*, directed by Andy and Larry Wachowski (Burbank, CA: Warner Brothers Pictures, 1999).

17. Oliver Wendell Holmes, "The Voiceless," 1858.

18. C. S. Lewis, "Christian Marriage," in *Mere Christianity*, accessed March 8, 2012, http://lib.ru/LEWISCL/mere_engl.txt. 1943.

19. Charles Colson, "The Lost Art of Commitment," *ChristianityToday.com*, accessed August 4, 2010, http://www.christianitytoday.com/ct/2010/august/10.49.html.

20. Robert Epstein, *Teen 2.0: Saving Our Children and Families from the Torment of Adolescence* (Fresno, CA: Linden Publishing, 2010).

21. "Just 15, He Leads Fight to Abolish Slavery," ABC News, accessed March 8, 2012, http://abcnews.go.com/GMA/story?id=2951434&page=1#.T1lynMwzJW4.

22. Seth Godin, "The Secret of the Web (Hint: It's a Virtue)," August 10, 2008, accessed March 8, 2012, http://sethgodin.typepad.com/seths_blog/2008/08/the-secret-of-t.html.

23. Jeremiah 6:16.

24. David Kinnaman, "5 Steps to a Better Career," *RELEVANTMagazine.com*, May 27, 2010, accessed March 8, 2012, http://www.relevantmagazine.com/life/career-money/features/21706-5-steps-to-a-better-career.

25. J. H. Wyman, *The Mexican*, directed by Gore Verbinski (Universal City, CA: DreamWorks, 2001).

26. Shauna Niequist, "Twenty-Five," in *Bittersweet: Thoughts on Change, Grace, and Learning the Hard Way* (Grand Rapids, MI: Zondervan, 2010).

27. John 21:18.

28. C. S. Lewis, "Christian Marriage," in *Mere Christianity*, accessed March 8, 2012, http://lib.ru/LEWISCL/mere_engl.txt. 1943.

29. Albert Torres, *Henry Poole Is Here*, directed by Mark Pellington (Beverly Hills, CA: Overture Films, 2008).

30. Isaiah 10:13.

31. Isaiah 10:15.

ACKNOWLEDGMENTS

A good book—which this one aspires to be—is never written in solitude. There is always a community behind it. Without a whole team of people, I would not have believed I had any words to share with the world, much less a book to write.

To all those who have spoken an encouraging word over the years or taken the time to read anything I've written, thank you. I'll do my best to mention as many of you as I can remember, but forgive me when I fail.

I am indebted to the uncanny patience and encouragement of my wife, Ashley. You've been bugging me to write a book for a while; thanks for believing in me when I didn't. Without you, there would be no writer, not to mention a book. In more ways than I can say, this book belongs to you.

To my parents—Keith and Robin—for teaching me the importance of good stories and for ultimately releasing me into the world to live one, thank you both. Marissa, Nikki, and Patrick:

you inspired this book without realizing it. If I could give my best advice as an older brother, it would be this book.

The missionaries, travelers, and troubadours I've met over the years—especially the staff of Adventures in Missions—have taught me so much through their stories and lives. To Seth Barnes for coaching, mentoring, and calling me out when I needed it. You helped me process many of the lessons and stories that made their way into this book. Thanks for seeing gifts in me before I recognized them myself. I'd like to thank Chris Reed, Paul Vasilko, David Lanning, and the rest of my friends at CTI Music Ministries, for forcing me to step up as a leader and learn what it means to wreck others.

To Michael Hyatt for constantly encouraging me to step out into my vocation, I am thankful. Mike, I owe much of my growth as a writer and communicator to your overwhelming generosity—thank you.

To my agent, friend, and coach, Mark Oestreicher, for provoking me to believe in myself, and the Youth Ministry Coaching Program (especially you, Paul), where I first announced I was a writer—thank you all. You rock.

To Randall Payleitner and the rest of the Moody team for taking a chance on a blogger pretending to be a writer, I'd like to say thanks. They are seriously some of the nicest people I know. Also, an honorable mention to Duane Sherman and his cadre of designers for not harming any tortoises in the making of this cover. Well done.

I'd be remiss if I didn't acknowledge Paul Cunningham for taking a risk with me in heading downtown on a whim one day to hang out with homeless people. Ed Cathey, Josh Darnell, and the staff at the Nashville Rescue Mission are saints that I aspire to be like . . . someday.

To Ron Ferguson, who will always be my pastor, and the family of Franklin Fellowship Church—thank you for showing me what it means to live a truly wrecked life, wherever I am.

To the readers of my blog and all the incredible people I've met online, I am forever grateful—without you guys, I'd have no business publishing anything.

Lastly, and most importantly, I am thankful to God—for wrecking my story and giving me a better one to live.

WHY HOLINESS MATTERS

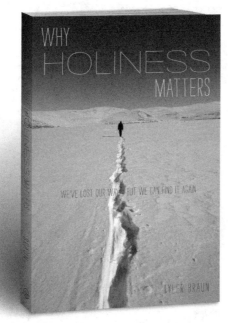

978-0-8024-0507-4

Our generation has little or no regard for holiness. And this makes sense given our misunderstanding of:

- Sin (we view it as either inevitable or we just go with it)
- Holiness (we view it as unrealistic or we ignore it because there's no immediate payoff)
- Innocence (we view it as subordinate to "experiencing the world")
- God (we often think He'll probably let us down—just like people do)

Instead of playing the "guilt/shame" card, Tyler Braun examines Jesus' example to recognize how His way of life contrasts the world's promises.

Also available as an eBook

MOODY
PUBLISHERS

www.MoodyPublishers.com

INCITING INCIDENTS

Inciting Incidents combines unique stories from eight creatives (artists, musicians, writers, thinkers, and leaders) managing the tensions between their faith, their place in life, and their work as artists. By capturing this next generation's battle between idealism and reality, these storytellers create understanding of those moments that truly shape us. Readers will be challenged to use their own art and their own life stories to find their way in God's Kingdom. The end result is that God has created each of us uniquely and we each have a growing part to play in His story.

Also available as an eBook

MOODY
PUBLISHERS
www.MoodyPublishers.com

HONEST TO GOD

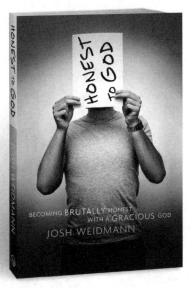

978-0-8024-0359-9

Is hypocrisy eroding your trust in relationships, the church, or even yourself? We long to know there is a God—and, yes, a community—who is big enough to accept us for who we are and loving enough not to leave us that way. Imagine how our relationships and witness would change if Christians everywhere began to live in a more authentic manner. Throughout the Bible, we find heroes of the faith who lived with daring, messy honesty before God and others. *Honest to God* is a practical and riveting study of biblical honesty. Follow next-generation author, Josh Weidmann, as he takes the reader on a journey toward true Christian authenticity. Both biblical and contemporary examples will give you practical principles and tools for self-examination that will lead to the freedom and transformation that come only through honesty.

Also available as an eBook

MOODY
PUBLISHERS

www.MoodyPublishers.com